AMONG THOSE BORN OF
WOMEN THERE WAS NONE
GREATER THAN JOHN

Among Those Born of Women There Was None Greater than John

Unveiling John the Baptist's True Mission

Jean-Jacques Trifault

Among Those Born of Women There Was None Greater
than John~Unveiling John the Baptist's True Mission
by Jean-Jacques Trifault
Copyright ©2011 by Jean-Jacques Trifault

Scriptures taken from the Holy Bible,
New International Version®, NIV®.
Copyright © 1984 by Biblica, Inc.™
Used by permission of Zondervan.
All rights reserved worldwide.
www.zondervan.com

First American Edition

Editors: Gabriela Neuwirth, Mary Trifault
Book cover and interior design: Kasia Krawczyk

Published by Footsteps To Wisdom Publishing
For questions and comments visit
www.footstepstowisdom.org

ISBN-13 978-0-9797877-9-9
ISBN-10 0-9797877-9-3

.

I f we look at the history of humankind, we can say it has largely developed and advanced because of the courage and the perseverance of men and women who did not hesitate to ask questions and to express their ideas, despite being misunderstood, rejected, and sometimes even experiencing fierce persecution during their lifetimes.

One such person was the 17th century Italian physicist and astronomer Galileo Galilei who supported the at-that-time revolutionary theory of Nicolaus Copernicus that the earth and other planets were revolving around the sun. He lived in an age when most of the world, having been taught the prevailing Catholic Church doctrine, believed that the earth was the center of the universe and that all the planets and stars, including the sun, revolved around the earth. Because of his controversial beliefs Galileo was branded a heretic and was brought before the Inquisition to renounce his views. Eventually, in fear for his life, he chose to deny his understanding.

The idea that Galileo supported was based on physical observations of the visible natural world, yet the group in power at that time dismissed his observations and the works of Copernicus. If Galileo, who promoted an idea that could be supported by physical evidence, was persecuted until he renounced his beliefs, how much more persecution could someone face who has been or is trying to present an unconventional idea that is completely invisible to our eyes?

Jesus' Invisible Idea

One of the persons who pursued this invisible field was Jesus Christ. He introduced new ways of how to live with God. Because during his lifetime the people around Jesus could not digest his new views, Jesus was labeled a heretic and intensely persecuted, and eventually he was killed.

We might ask ourselves where the people got the power to persecute Jesus to such an extent when he was just speaking about something that they could not perceive. Did this power come from human beings alone, or is it possible that there was another force coming from the invisible realm of existence beyond, and that this is the reason he had to endure such strong opposition?

Even today, if we approach certain groups of people, like Christian ministers, with a rather innocent question such as, "Why did Jesus die so young?", we might perceive a defensive reaction, an attempt to give some quick answer or even a rejection of our question. Such a quick response from a minister can make us assume that he has faced this question before, and if he accepts to reply to our question, it seems he has learned the answer from another authority. Or, if the minister does not have a good answer, he might not hesitate to say, "There is no need to ask this kind of question. This was God's Will. This is what we believe." After such responses, coupled with tense emotions, we surely would not wish to present another similar inquiry. According to this experience, if we decide to present questions to people who consider themselves to be religious, we should be ready to face resistance and even persecution.

THE IMPORTANCE OF ASKING QUESTIONS AND LOOKING FOR ANSWERS

Let us take a closer look at the ones who question as well as the ones who respond to questions.

As we observe someone who poses a question, we notice that the topic of his inquiry as well as his manner of asking is connected to the level of development of his character. For example, when we are young our questions and the answers we seek are quite simple. As we grow and our interests develop, we discover deeper aspects of life and our questions become more profound. Based on the development of both our mind and our interests we might eventually arrive to the place where our questions coincide with the complex questions asked by some of those who lived before us.

As well, if we come to the point of questioning something that our ancestors who have left this earth did not question and we discover a suitable answer to our dilemma, we might experience a lot of resistance coming from within ourselves to accept the answer, even though there is no resistance coming from others around us. This resistance comes from our history, holding us to the views of our ancestors. Nevertheless it is important to know, even though we might pass through a tornado of emotions by asking certain questions and receiving certain answers, as we open ourselves to those questions and answers, we advance to a higher state of mind.

At the same time, regardless we might be happy to arrive to a level where we have all kinds of questions, if those whom we question have decided to stop their search for answers, we should be prepared to face opposition and persecution from these persons, the same as other people before us faced all kinds of opposition. In this sense, it is good to be aware that if people have difficulties to listen to us, it is not because our question is strange, but because this question or this field represents a great challenge for the one whom we ask. It is for this reason, when we are at the age of entering adulthood, some people will tell us, "Do not talk about certain subjects in public because you are not going to be liked."

But despite unwelcoming reactions from within us or outside of us, the reality is that it is important to ask questions because it is an essential way to broaden and to develop our minds. Based on the questions coming to us we can assess our internal growth, whether we have advanced and become more rounded or we have regressed and become narrower. And if we find ourselves in the position to listen to different questions, the way we react, if we are defensive and aggressive or if we are peaceful, reveals where we stand and what direction of development our characters have been taking.

Indeed, the thousands of years of human history were paved with a multitude of questions to which a multitude of answers were given. And the more history progressed based on different discoveries, the more human beings developed. If there was a time when people stopped to strive for answers or gave up on ideals of achieving a greater goal for themselves and others, surely these people and all their generation found themselves stagnating and eventually regressing to a darker age.

In this regard, if someone poses a question, we can look at this person in the context of history and see him as passing through a certain period of history when this question has been asked as well, or we can see him as encountering a question that has not yet been asked in all of history. Instead of persecuting the one who questions a certain issue that has not yet been touched upon, it would be wise to try to find an answer to his question, or at least allow that question to be heard. If everyone took this attitude and if all different kinds of questions and answers freely circulated through the course of history, surely humankind would advance at a higher speed.

Questions that Children Ask

This openness to questions starts with our attitude toward our young children who ask why the sun is disappearing at night and coming back in the morning. Instead of pushing their question away or taking it lightly, we should be happy with the question and eager to answer. We might recall that a long time ago someone who posed a similar question as these children, wondering if the sun was turning around the earth or the earth was turning around the sun, was in danger of having his blood shed for the audacity of his inquiry.

Therefore, if today we have the pleasure to find the answers to certain difficult questions quickly and effortlessly without finding ourselves living a miserable life as a result of our questions, we need to be aware this is because there is a foundation made by others before us. They accepted to go through a multitude of difficulties in search of a reply, possibly being considered strange by the ones living around them and therefore having a lonely life. Based on their sufferings, years later we have answers that come to our heads so easily, like nuts falling from the trees onto the grass. Because of all these people from previous centuries who accepted to endure all kinds of threats, to the point of being killed, we now can pass with ease through a process of questioning and receiving many answers, as if we were passing through history in a short time.

Can we remember how many questions we have asked and how many answers have been given to us in our lifetimes? If by now we have come to a place where we find resistance to our questions, we can consider that we have arrived at the point where we are able to challenge the knowledge so far accumulated throughout history.

We Are Historical People

So indeed, in the sense that we all can access the combined knowledge of history and benefit from this knowledge in all different ways—mentally, emotionally and materially—we can say we are historical people and that we are the fruit of history. Based on this intellectual inheritance new questions can be raised, in hope that, as we are given freedom to pursue the answers to these questions, we ourselves and humankind can reach higher and higher levels of evolution.

As we view ourselves as the fruits of history, the question that arises is if we really comprehend the importance of such a position. And if we reach this awareness, can we see the importance of our lives, of our everyday decisions, in regard to history and ultimately in regard to God, who is the driving force behind creating a history of goodness?

People can impact the history of God in two kinds of ways: they can benefit God's history or they can put God's history in danger due to their lack of understanding of their historical positions. As well, they might come to the point where they believe they are gods themselves, having the power to manipulate history according to their wishes, disregarding the accumulated ancestral merit they stand upon.

In this sense, as humans we can either overvalue ourselves or deny our historical value and in this way be unaware of the effects that our thoughts and actions can have on the present time and on the future. And as we who represent the past, the present and the future make wrong choices, we can inflict a lot of damage on the present and future and destroy the foundation of goodness accumulated by the sacrifices of those of the past.

One very important and influential time for the course of God's history took place place two thousand years ago, when Jesus Christ, called the Son of God, was living on this earth. Nevertheless, do you think that his followers and the people living around him knew how important they were? Did they understand that the choices they made in relation to Jesus would bring them to a better place, to the point they could reach the stage of development where God could love them or, contrary to that, that their choices could bring them to a place where they would find themselves abandoned by God, a stage that was completely against the wishes of their hearts and thus against the will of God?

How about us? Are we aware that based on our choices we can move history forward to a better and more prosperous place of existence or backwards to a darker and more hostile place?

Knowing that the knowledge we have accumulated belongs to our ancestors and knowing that the beliefs by which we conduct our lives create history and ultimately influence the will of God Who seeks to bring about a history of goodness, we need to ask ourselves before God, "Have we as human beings held onto the knowledge that has been discovered so far and seen this as our primary value, or can we accept to move to new dimensions of knowledge, knowledge that finally allows God to dwell within and among ourselves?"

JOHN THE BAPTIST AS A HISTORICAL PERSON

During the time of Jesus there was one man who had a crucial role in history. His name was John, referred to by many as John the Baptist.

To give a brief account of his life, according to the records in the Bible we are told that during his lifetime he was a man who was most revered and admired in Israel, to the point that many people, including the priests, thought that he was the Christ, as recorded in Jn 1:19-21: *"Now this was John's testimony when the Jews of Jerusalem sent priests and Levites to ask him who he was. He did not fail to confess, but confessed freely, 'I am not the Christ.' They asked him, 'Then who are you? Are you Elijah?' He said, 'I am not.' 'Are you the Prophet?' He answered, 'No.'"*

Nevertheless, even though it seemed that John had been important for God, we are also told that at some stage in his life he became the least important. This is what we hear Jesus saying about John in Mt 11:11: *"I tell you the truth: Among those born of women there has not risen anyone greater than John the Baptist; yet he who is the least in heaven is greater than he."* The one who once had the highest authority seems to have lost it all.

What could have possibly happened to John, who seemed to have known God so well? In the Bible it says that John spent many years in the wilderness trying to build a relationship with God. However, in spite of his long years of training he struggled to recognize God in Jesus Christ after they finally met. In Mk 1:10 we read that John received a sign from God in the form of a dove descending on Jesus on the fine morning he baptized Jesus in the Jordan River, *"As Jesus was coming up out of the water, he* (John) *saw heaven being torn open and the Spirit descending on him* (Jesus) *like a dove."* Yet in spite of this, John did not become a disciple of Jesus. He chose to go his own road instead, turning his back on Jesus, and in doing so he also turned his back on God.

Maybe Jesus wanted to make John understand the importance of his position, that John as a priest stood on the foundation of many prophets who had come before him and suffered a multitude of persecutions in order to elevate the knowledge of God. Using this viewpoint, we can say that when John failed to follow Jesus, at the same time John abandoned all the knowledge of history that had allowed him to recognize the love of God that Jesus carried when John first met him at the Jordan River.

Although there are no other historical records, besides a few phrases here and there, that tell us what Jesus and John could have talked about in their time together at the Jordan River, we can guess that Jesus must have tried to witness to John in many different ways. Nevertheless, no matter how many conversations there might have been, in the end John concluded, *"He* (Jesus) *must become greater, I must become less."* (Jn 3:30) Even though considered by many as an act of humility, John's statement and his choice to not follow Jesus determined the choice of the whole nation, and consequently whether the course of history was to become one of prosperity or one of destruction. As mentioned above, due to his position as a religious leader, John was not just one of the many other citizens who encountered Jesus in their lifetime. John represented the foundation of many people who had endured suffering in order to understand and advance the knowledge of God. For this reason it is said in Jn 1:6-7, *"There came a man who was sent from God; his name was John. He came as a witness to testify concerning that light, so that through him all men might believe."*

John had been called by God to fulfill a specific mission to testify about the light who was Jesus and then to be loyal to that light, so that through John everyone could recognize and follow the light as well. Based on his foundation John was able to initially recognize the light. When after that John rejected the light, not only his own destiny changed, as illustrated in Mt 14:10 *"and* (Herod) *had John beheaded in prison,"* but also the destiny of the people of his nation was put in jeopardy, which we can see from the historical records that tell us about the harsh treatments that were inflicted by the Romans on the Jewish people after Jesus' death. Furthermore, because John did not recognize Jesus as the Son of God, God's desire to bring all human beings to a place where they could experience His love to the fullest degree could not be realized in that time. John's unfortunate choice not only blocked him but blocked everyone from entering the Kingdom of Heaven that Jesus wanted to build in his time.

Maybe if John had more seriously understood his responsibility in the fulfillment of God's will, he would have been more careful about the choices he made. His decision of going his own way caused him to become the least in heaven and he was unable to make straight the way of the Lord, as he had once prophesied to the religious leaders in Jn 1:23, *"John replied in the words of Isaiah the prophet, 'I am the voice of one calling in the desert, 'Make straight the way for the Lord.'"* By failing his mission, John not only brought about his own downfall but, as he descended into darkness, he took the whole world with him.

God Had Designated John for Something Special

Already before John was born there were signs that made people believe God had designated John for something special. When John's father Zachariah doubted the angel Gabriel's message that a son would be born to him, he became mute until the birth of his son and the fulfillment of his agreement to name him John. (Lk 1:20, 1:63-64) Witnessing these events, *"All the neighbors were all filled with awe, and throughout the hill country of Judea people were talking about all these things. Everyone who heard this wondered about it, asking, 'What then is this child going to be?' For the Lord's hand was with him."* (Lk 1:65-66)

Then Lk 1:76-77 brings us Zachariah's song commemorating John's birth: *"And you, my child, will be called a prophet of the Most High; for you will go on before the Lord to prepare the way for him, to give his people the knowledge of salvation through the forgiveness of their sins."*

By the time John had grown up he was well known throughout the country: *"And so John came, baptizing in the desert region and preaching a baptism of repentance for the forgiveness of sins. The whole Judean countryside and all the people of Jerusalem went out to him. Confessing their sins, they were baptized by him in the Jordan River. John wore clothing made of camel's hair, with a leather belt around his waist, and he ate locusts and wild honey."* (Mk 1:4-6) The rabbis of his time came to respect John as a great person. They were aware of the signs at his birth and saw that he was able to draw large crowds and ignite the people through his preaching, much better than they themselves could. John had lived in the desert for some time alone, like a hermit, searching for answers to his questions. With time John must have found the answers that he wanted to convey to the Israelites, which at some point he began to preach to the people, as described in Lk 1:80: *"And the child grew and became strong in spirit; and he lived in the desert until he appeared publicly to Israel."*

JOHN'S SEARCH FOR ANSWERS

In order to receive a new message from God, John must have been aggressive in his search for the answers that had not yet been presented. He was not content with just repeating the words that already had been preached, hoping that they would eventually bring people to the light. Instead, he accepted to humble himself before God, in hope of receiving some new

understanding from Him. And based on his efforts to com-
municate with the God of Moses and Abraham, John must
have discovered that God indeed heard the ones who cried
out to Him with humility. As John developed the nature of
listening for answers instead of just trying to interpret what
he did not comprehend, his knowledge became quite different from what had been discovered thus far.

He realized that simply reading and memorizing the
Scriptures over and over and being faithful to the words
that had been given in the past was not enough for achieving purification of sin. The rituals of atonement that his
religion was presenting, like animal offerings and the multitude of other ceremonies, seemed to John slightly outdated.
After many years in the wilderness looking for new insights,
John succeeded in becoming the most fervent preacher of
his nation. He gained a large following of people who were
convinced that John had reached an elevated level of spiri-
tuality, which they could not see in other religious leaders.
John's teachings may have inspired many to begin ascetic
lives in the wilderness in search of a deeper relationship
with God.

Because John was so knowledgeable in God's word and
understood its importance, he wanted to give the word to
everyone, believing that knowledge of the word and faith in
the word would bring a revival to the entire nation. However,
John knew that the word alone was not enough to remove
the sin of the people. To prepare them for the time when
they could be completely free from sin he began to introduce

the rite of baptism, a ceremony for the cleansing of sin, and he preached about repentance: *"In those days John the Baptist came, preaching in the Desert of Judea and saying, 'Repent, for the kingdom of heaven is near."* (Mt 3:1)

Just the Voice Calling in the Wilderness?

John surely must have believed that God was very close to him, since God gave him many inspirations and helped him to speak to those who came to see him. When the priests saw large crowds that came to listen to John and were inspired by John's word, they looked up to him, as in fact they believed he might be the Messiah whom they had been waiting for, or at least a great prophet. At the same time we can see that John showed some disregard for the religious leadership, calling them a 'brood of vipers': *"But when he saw many of the Pharisees and Sadducees coming to where he was baptizing, he said to them: 'You brood of vipers! Who warned you to flee from the coming wrath?'"* (Mt 3:7)

Seeing the impact John had on the people of his time we can believe that he must have been questioning himself, "Am I indeed just the voice calling in the wilderness preparing the way for someone greater to come, or am I the one God was promising to send?" Finding himself on the top of the pyramid of his society, at a place where he was looked upon with such high regard by everyone around him, it is easy to imagine that John was tempted to believe that he was the Promised One they thought him to be.

Nevertheless, at the same time John was aware that the rite of baptism that he offered to people could not completely absolve people of their sin. For this reason he kept proclaiming, *"I baptize you with water for repentance. But after me will come one who is more powerful than I, whose sandals I am not fit to carry. He will baptize you with the Holy Spirit and with fire."* (Mt 3:11)

Tʜᴇ Pʀᴏᴘʜᴇᴄʏ ᴏғ Jᴇꜱᴜꜱ' Bɪʀᴛʜ

After discussing some part of the life of John, let us now look at the life of Jesus. Long before the birth of Jesus, the prophet Isaiah announced Jesus' coming to the nation of Israel: *"For to us a child is born, to us a son is given, and the government will be on his shoulders. And he will be called Wonderful Counselor, Mighty God, Everlasting Father, Prince of Peace. Of the increase of his government and peace there will be no end. He will reign on David's throne and over his kingdom, establishing and upholding it with justice and righteousness from that time on and forever. The zeal of the LORD Almighty will accomplish this."* (Isa 9:6-7)

Based on this early prophecy of Jesus' birth and his mission given to the people of Israel, we can surely say that it had been for quite a long time that God was preparing the nation of Israel as the place where He intended to establish His Kingdom.

And as the story tells us, when this time finally arrived, it was in the sixth month after Elizabeth had become pregnant with John. At that time an angel came to Elizabeth's relative, Mary, and said to her, *"You will be with child and give birth to a son, and you are to give him the name Jesus. He will be great and will be called the Son of the Most High. The Lord God will give him the throne of his father David, and he will reign over the house of Jacob forever; his kingdom will never end."* (Lk 1:31-33)

When Mary was wondering how this could be, the angel explained to her, *"The Holy Spirit will come upon you, and the power of the Most High will overshadow you. So the holy one to be born will be called the Son of God. Even Elizabeth your relative is going to have a child in her old age, and she who was said to be barren is in her sixth month."* (Lk 1:35-36) This is the first indication that the destiny of the baby of Elizabeth, who would be John, and the destiny of the baby of her relative Mary, who would be Jesus, might be connected.

After this message from God, Mary decided to visit Elizabeth. When Mary entered Zachariah's house and greeted Elizabeth, *"... the baby leaped in her* (Elizabeth's) *womb, and Elizabeth was filled with the Holy Spirit. In a loud voice she exclaimed: 'Blessed are you among women, and blessed is the child you will bear!'"* (Lk 1:41-42) Thereafter, *"Mary stayed with Elizabeth for about three months and then returned home."* (Lk 1:56)

Dangers Surrounding Jesus' Birth

This is the account of Jesus' birth according to the book of Matthew: *"This is how the birth of Jesus Christ came about: His mother Mary was pledged to be married to Joseph, but before they came together, she was found to be with child through the Holy*

Spirit. Because Joseph her husband was a righteous man and did not want to expose her to public disgrace, he had in mind to divorce her quietly." (Mt 1:18-19) In this dangerous and crucial time for Jesus' fate an angel appeared to Joseph in a dream, instructing him *"... Joseph son of David, do not be afraid to take Mary home as your wife, because what is conceived in her is from the Holy Spirit."*(Mt 1:20)

However, dangers continued to surround Jesus and soon after Jesus was born Joseph received a new warning from an angel: *"When they* (the Magi who had been told about Jesus' birth through a star) *had gone, an angel of the Lord appeared to Joseph in a dream. 'Get up,' he said, 'take the child and his mother and escape to Egypt. Stay there until I tell you, for Herod is going to search for the child to kill him.'"* (Mt 2:13-14)

They stayed in exile until the news of Herod's death reached Mary and Joseph. They decided that it was safe then to go back to Israel and to raise Jesus there. *"So he* (Joseph) *got up, took the child and his mother and went to the land of Israel. But when he heard that Archelaus was reigning in Judea in place of his father Herod, he was afraid to go there. Having been warned in a dream, he withdrew to the district of Galilee, in a town called Nazareth. So was fulfilled what was said through the prophets: 'He will be called a Nazarene.'"* (Mt 2:21-23)

From these records we can see that the circumstances of Jesus' birth caused a lot of fear and discomfort among people, compared to John's birth, which is portrayed as quite glorious and miraculous, with his father Zachariah becoming mute until John's birth. (Lk 1:63-66)

Furthermore, John's parents stayed at their home in Judea, in comparison to Jesus' parents who moved with him many times. After Mary had visited the house of Zachariah in the Judean hill country and became pregnant, she went back to Galilee. (Lk 1:56) Then she came back with Joseph to Bethlehem in Judea when a census was being taken and everyone had to go to his or her hometown to register: *"So Joseph also went up from the town of Nazareth in Galilee to Judea, to Bethlehem the town of David, because he belonged to the house and line of David."* (Lk 2:4-5) Once Jesus had been born in Bethlehem and his life came to be in jeopardy, as we have discussed, Mary and Joseph left for Egypt, where they stayed until they came back and settled in Nazareth in Galilee.

In the midst of all these tumultuous circumstances, God gave visions to different people about the greatness of Jesus, maybe in hope that some of these persons might protect him as a child. As we have stated above, before Jesus' conception Elizabeth was given a special vision when her relative Mary visited her. (Lk 1:41-45) Then, the shepherds in the hills close to the manger where Jesus was born were visited by an angel bringing good news: *"Do not be afraid. I bring you good news of great joy that will be for all the people. Today in the town of David a Savior has been born to you; he is Christ the Lord."* (Lk 2:10-11) As well, Magi from the East received a sign about the birth of someone special. They went to the palace of King Herod and asked, *"Where is the one who has been born king of the Jews? We saw his star in the east and have come to worship him."* (Mt 2:2) But for some reason, instead of rejoicing, *"When King*

Herod heard this he was disturbed, and all Jerusalem with him." (Mt 2:3)

After Jesus had been circumcised, Mary and Joseph went with him to Jerusalem to offer him officially as their first-born to God, as was asked by the Jewish law. At that time Mary and Joseph met a righteous and holy man, called Simeon, who somehow had been waiting for the Christ. When Simeon saw Mary and Joseph with Jesus, *"Then Simeon blessed them and said to Mary, his mother: 'This child is destined to cause the falling and rising of many in Israel, and to be a sign that will be spoken against.'"* (Lk 2:34) In that moment a prophetess called Anna, who had been living an ascetic lifestyle, approached and as stated in Lk 2:38, *"Coming up to them at that very moment, she gave thanks to God and spoke about the child to all who were looking forward to the redemption of Jerusalem."*

Indeed, all these people who had received revelations and visions about Jesus just seemed to be happy to finally have met him. However, after they testified about him, there are no longer any records about them. This means, like so many times in Jesus' life, after the moment that some people had been waiting for all their lives had come and they were in front of the one who could liberate them from their bondage of sin, they just rejoiced for a short while and then they went back to their daily lives as if nothing had ever happened.

We have very few records about Jesus when he was a young boy. One of the few accounts is given in Lk 2:41-42, stating that *"Every year his parents went to Jerusalem for the Feast of the Passover. When he (Jesus) was twelve years old, they went up to the Feast, according to the custom."* On their way home his parents realized that Jesus was not with them and they went back to Jerusalem, where as recorded in Lk 2:46-47, *"After three days they found him in the temple courts, sitting among the teachers, listening to them and asking them questions. Everyone who heard him was amazed at his understanding and his answers."*

After this event, we are only told in Lk 2:52, *"And Jesus grew in wisdom and stature, and in favor with God and men."* Compared to John, who at an early age went into the desert, preaching and baptizing and attracting all of the people in Judea and beyond, (Mt 3:5) Jesus, after the turmoil at his birth, seemed to have grown up in the shadows of Galilee, until the fateful meeting between him and John.

JOHN MEETS JESUS AT THE JORDAN RIVER

According to the record in the Bible this meeting took place sometime during the month of April when the heat of the desert was not yet too strong. While John was baptizing people, preparing them for the coming of the Lord, someone special approached him and asked to be baptized by him. This person was Jesus. In that moment, John, who had seen so many people of all kinds of stature, suddenly hesitated, as recorded in (Mt 3:14): *"But John tried to deter him, saying, 'I need to be baptized by you, and do you come to me?"*

From the multitude of human beings that had passed before his eyes to be baptized, this was the first time that John found himself saying to someone, "I, John, cannot baptize you." He would not even say it to the King or to the High Priest because if he did, it would mean that John would have to place them in a higher position than John himself. And if such a person was a religious leader, John would be compelled to follow him as his spiritual leader and guide. Instead we see John calling the priesthood 'a brood of vipers' (Mt 3:7) who needed to repent of their sins, clearly showing that John did not have a high regard for people of leadership and power, even the religious ones. However, that all changed when Jesus came to be baptized by John.

In order for John to distinguish Jesus from all the people he had met so far, we can deduce that John could perceive who was clean and who was unclean. This ability demonstrates that John had a soul that was highly developed, a quality that he must have been able to achieve through the years of his spiritual training when he was living in the desert. (Lk 1:80) All this preparation allowed him to sense if the person who presented himself was spiritually less pure, equally pure, or as John experienced in this moment when he saw Jesus, purer than him. Furthermore, John could perceive himself speaking differently when Jesus came to him and asked to be baptized; John right away responded to him that he, John, needed to be baptized by Jesus instead.

We might question why Jesus came all the way from Galilee in the north to Jordan in order to visit John. Did Jesus simply come to see his relative?

From Jesus' response to John in Mt 3:15 *"'Let it be so now; it is proper for us to do this to fulfill all righteousness.' ...,"* we realize that they both appeared to know the scriptures very well. And, indeed, when Jesus spoke to John in this way, John accepted to baptize Jesus. Still, in that moment John was aware that Jesus was not like everyone else who came to receive forgiveness of his or her sins through him. Based on what had come out of his mouth when he saw Jesus, John started to understand that Jesus could offer the baptism that would truly forgive sin, his sin as well as the sin of the people.

JOHN'S PROMISE OF THE FORGIVENESS OF SIN

People traveled from all over the nation to be baptized by John. Knowing that for a long time God had been preparing the nation of Israel by sending many prophets, we can believe that He must have had a great plan for John in order to endow him with so much authority. Seeing the Israelites being so attracted to and so fascinated by John, we can say that God was not only seeking to elevate John to a higher level of understanding by giving revelations to him, but God also wanted to lift the people and to wake them up through John, as God had wanted to do through so many prophets before him.

Indeed, people did not come on foot or donkey to the Jordan River to participate in yet another festival there, but they came because they wanted to remove the sickness, called sin, that was rooted deep within them. John promised forgiveness of sin, at least to some degree, through baptism and repentance. This event is portrayed in Mk 1:4-5 as, *"And so John came, baptizing in the desert region and preaching a baptism of repentance for the forgiveness of sins. The whole Judean countryside and all the people of Jerusalem went out to him. Confessing their sins, they were baptized by him in the Jordan River."*

And so, many people made a pilgrimage to the Jordan River where John was, coming from the far north of Galilee and the far south of Judea in hopes of having their sins forgiven. For many this meant to have their sins removed entirely, even though as they were baptized by John with the water from the Jordan River, he said to them as recorded in Mk 1:8, *"I baptize you with water, but he will baptize you with the Holy Spirit."*

Based on how many people came to see John, we can believe he must have repeated this sentence quite many times. The reciting of this message must have made him more aware that someone would come after him and that this someone would present something much more powerful than water. Nevertheless it is doubtful how much his followers understood the meaning of this sentence. We can be sure that many of them thought the rite of baptism would completely cut off their sins and that the water John was using, which symbolized purification, had the ability to dissolve all the dirt that sin had created within their bodies.

While John was carrying out the rite of baptism by the Jordan River he was leading a humble life, as Mt 3:4

describes: *"John's clothes were made of camel's hair, and he had a leather belt around his waist. His food was locusts and wild honey."* It seemed that through his external appearance John wanted to stress the importance of living a humble lifestyle, since he knew that the water he baptized the people with would not completely dissolve or evaporate their sin and that they as well as John himself were still open to temptations. Therefore, even though John had the power to forgive sin to some degree, he felt the necessity to live an austere life in order to be able to maintain purity and keep devotion to God.

UNDERSTANDING THE CONCEPT OF SIN

How well did John understand the concept of sin? He might have thought one of the characteristics of sin was the desire for fine food and therefore he ate only locusts and wild honey. As well, thinking that another expression of sin was a desire for material goods, John abandoned fine clothing and began to wear camel skin.

But John must have had another understanding that sin was also connected to something within our flesh that has been passed on from generation to generation, ultimately connecting us to the original seducer, the serpent from the Garden of Eden or a 'viper'. Calling religious leaders a 'brood of vipers', John also mentioned about the coming wrath of judgment *"... You brood of vipers! Who warned you to flee from the coming wrath?"* (Lk 3:7) John was clearly aware that the sin we all carry buried deeply in our flesh could only be removed by the judgment of someone greater than him.

John also emphasized, *"Produce fruit in keeping with repentance. And do not think you can say to yourselves, 'We have Abraham as our father.' I tell you that out of these stones God can raise up children for Abraham. The ax is already at the root of the trees, and every tree that does not produce good fruit will be cut down and thrown into the fire."* (Mt 3:8-10) He made people around him aware that, contrary to their beliefs, they did not come from the lineage of Abraham, which was the lineage of God, but from the lineage of the enemy of God, the viper. For this reason, in order to carry the lineage of goodness and produce good fruits, which is to become children of goodness, people needed to go through a process of purification that would separate them from the lineage of the devil, with which they were connected. And it seemed that this was meant to happen soon.

When John predicted the coming of the special person who would perform this task, saying, *"I baptize you with water for repentance. But after me will come one who is more powerful than I, whose sandals I am not fit to carry. He will baptize you with the Holy Spirit and with fire,"* (Mt 3:11) he included himself with those who needed to be redeemed since 'he was not worthy to carry this one's sandals'. Preparing everyone to meet this special person, John stressed the attitude of humility necessary to welcome the one who would bring God's judgment to the world. Regardless of John's knowledge and his respected status in society, when the one who could bring the true baptism would come, meaning the one who could truly cut the people's connection to the lineage of sin, John could only look upon that person with deep humility.

JOHN'S VISION OF THE DOVE

When Jesus presented himself before John at the Jordan River, John humbly accepted to baptize Jesus. In that moment John was very much in awe of Jesus. His admiration helped him to be open to a special vision of a holy spirit descending upon Jesus in the form of a dove: *"As soon as Jesus was baptized, he went up out of the water. At that moment heaven was opened, and he saw the Spirit of God descending like a dove and lighting on him."* (Mt 3:16) Then John heard a voice from heaven, *"This is my Son, whom I love; with him I am well pleased."* (Mt 3:17). Amazed by what was taking place, in this moment John must have realized that the one he had prophesied about was no longer an idea or a concept, but had become real with the coming of Jesus and with the dove who was with him.

Indeed, Jesus did not come to praise his cousin John for what he was doing, but by his coming Jesus asked John to make a very important choice, a choice that would determine John's own destiny as well as humankind's destiny. But did the mental and emotional impact that John had experienced in this short, miraculous moment stay with him or did it fade away as John busied himself with taking care of the people who were anxiously awaiting their turn to be baptized, probably showing restlessness and fatigue for having had to wait? Surely, in comparison to the amount of time John had been spending to baptize people, the moment during which he had met Jesus was very short. So, what did John do after this short and yet so crucial moment?

JESUS WAS THE LIGHT

As we read the account in Jn 1:1-4, *"In the beginning was the Word, and the Word was with God, and the Word was God. He was with God in the beginning. Through him all things were made; without him nothing was made that has been made. In him was life, and the life was the light of men,"* we might feel that John the Baptist heard similar words when he met Jesus at the Jordan River and received a vision about him. Indeed, in that moment John the Baptist must have understood that a new beginning would come through Jesus. Furthermore, when encountering Jesus and seeing the life he carried within him, it must have become obvious to John that compared to Jesus everyone else seemed to have no life. And when he asked Jesus to baptize him instead of he, John, baptizing Jesus, John must have perceived the hope Jesus represented for him and therefore also for humankind, that through Jesus he and everyone else could be resurrected to life.

John might have also been aware that it would be difficult for the people who were caught in their misery to recognize the light and that he needed to open their eyes to the light that had come, as it is said in Jn 1:5-7: *"The light shines in the darkness, but the darkness has not understood it. There came a man who was sent from God; his name was John. He came as a witness concerning the light, so that through him all men might believe."*

Indeed, God had prepared John more than any of the religious people of his time. Based on John's ascetic lifestyle, his humble search for a deeper understanding of the scriptures, and his efforts to create a relationship with God, God endowed John with special wisdom. John used this wisdom to guide those who came to him for counsel about how to live a life of purity and how to prepare for the One who was coming. In Lk 3:11 we read about John advising the people, *"The man with two tunics should share with him who has none, and the one who has food should do the same,"* and in Lk 3:12-14, *"Tax collectors also came to be baptized. 'Teacher,' they asked, 'what should we do?' 'Don't collect any more than you are required to,' he told them. Then some soldiers asked him, 'And what should we do?' He replied, 'Don't extort money and don't accuse people falsely—be content with your pay.'"*

Judging from his words directed to the people, asking them to be generous and honest in preparation for meeting the Lord to come, and considering John's austere lifestyle, John must have spoken based on what he himself had done. He must have been a person who was aware of his daily actions, checking whether his actions allowed God to come closer to him or if they moved him further away from God. In time, John was able to come closer and closer into the light, which in turn led him to recognize the one who carried the light. It was God's hope that John could testify about his experience when he met this person. As described in Jn 1:8,

"He himself was not the light; he came only as a witness to the light." This means, even though John distinguished himself from the multitudes of people who were in darkness, he was not the light himself; there was something in him that made him similar to the people. He was able to give light to them, but he still carried darkness within him.

Then with Jesus' appearance, the true light that gives light to every man was coming into the world. (Jn 1:9) If John was able to perceive the true light and glorify that light in front of the people who were following him, the darkness could be removed from him, and all those who followed him would also be able to see the light. And if they humbled themselves and received the light, the darkness of sin could be removed from them as well. Subsequently they all could be elevated to come into the position of God's children: *"Yet to all who received him* (Jesus), *to those who believed in his name, he gave the right to become children of God."* (Jn 1:12)

The One to Prepare the Way for the Lord

The question is whether John helped in the fulfillment of this hopeful prophecy. In order for this prophecy to be realized, John needed to live up to the prophecy of Isaiah, as stated in Mk 1:2-3: *"It is written in Isaiah the prophet: 'I will send my messenger ahead of you, who will prepare your way – a voice of one calling in the desert, 'Prepare the way for the Lord, make straight paths for him.'"* Therefore, was John just a voice crying in the wilderness, or was he more than that, did he indeed make the path straight for the one who was the true light? Let us see what the story tells us.

John was aware of Isaiah's prophecy. He told the priests who were questioning him that he was neither the Christ nor Elijah nor the Prophet and, when they further pressed him for an answer, he *"replied in the words of Isaiah the prophet, 'I am the voice of the one calling in the desert, 'Make straight the way for the Lord.'"* (Jn 1:23) In Jn 1:26-27 John tells the Pharisees who were wondering why then he baptized, *"I baptize with water, but among you stands one you do not know. He is the one who comes after me, the thongs of whose sandals I am not worthy to untie."* And in Lk 3:16 it is written that John answered the people who were questioning him if he was the Christ: *"I baptize you with water. But one more powerful than I will come … He will baptize you with the Holy Spirit and with fire."* It seems that up until this point John understood his position as a messenger heralding the arrival of the Christ, but the question remains whether, when the one whose arrival John was announcing had come, would John understand what it meant 'to make straight the way for the Lord'?

CARRYING THE LINEAGE OF DEATH

When John was accusing the priests of carrying the blood of vipers, (Mt 3:7) he as the son of the high priest must have known that this stained blood was also in his veins. This must have been one of the reasons he understood that he was not the Lord or the Christ and thus he constantly spoke about

someone coming who was more powerful than him. Therefore, even though in the scriptures we cannot find any clear
statement that tells us about John's belief concerning his own
lineage, based on his testimonies about the one who would be
born of the lineage of life, we can assume he must have seen
himself being more connected to the lineage of death or the
lineage of the viper. Consequently, like everyone, he needed to
be reborn as a child coming from the lineage of God, which
as explained in Jn 1:13 would make them *"children born not of
natural descent, nor of human decision or a husband's will, but
born of God."* And in order to become a child of God, John,
like everyone, needed to receive the one who carried life and
to believe in him: *"Yet to all those who received him, to those who
believed in his name, he gave the right to become children of God."*
(Jn 1:12)

As we understand that the one who carried life or light
came to eliminate the darkness that came from the lineage of
the viper, and that the people needed to keep faith in him in
order for their lineage to be changed, we realize that darkness would not just disappear automatically with the coming
of the light. If darkness would simply vanish once the light
approached, then just by Jesus passing through the land of Israel, the souls of the people would have been transformed into
brightness in an instant, since he carried the light of God. If
the darkness existing within the nature of human beings could
be expelled in this way, then during the time Jesus was alive all
the land of Israel could have been illuminated, especially when
we know how much Jesus traveled throughout the country.

How Was Darkness Created?

How was darkness created in the first place? If we study the fall of human beings, we become aware that the darkness came about because at the very beginning of creation the serpent corrupted human beings who were meant to carry the nature of God or the nature of light. Therefore, to remove this darkness, the ones who are corrupted with the nature of the serpent need to welcome the one who brings the light, reversing the action of the fall.

God prepared John as the representative of darkness to achieve this incredible task. It was for this reason that He asked John to abandon his secular status as the son of the high priest and move into the wilderness. When John agreed to take this road, God revealed Himself to John in different ways, giving him revelations and training him to have faith by instructing him to baptize with water.

Furthermore, at the same time as John was educated by God internally and externally, God also told him that besides him someone else would come, and this one would carry the light and be called God's son.

John's Testimony

When Jesus came to be baptized by John, John saw the heaven opening and the Holy Spirit who had become flesh together with Jesus. He heard God calling Jesus his Son. This event is recorded in Lk 3:21-22 as, *"When all the people were being baptized, Jesus was baptized too. And as he was praying, heaven was opened and the Holy Spirit descended on him in bodily form like a dove. And a voice came from heaven: 'You are my Son, whom I love; with you I am well pleased.'"* This same event is described in Jn 1:32: *"Then John gave this testimony: 'I saw the Spirit come down from heaven as a dove and remain on him.'"* Furthermore, in Jn 1:33 it is said that John admitted, *"I would not have known him, except that the one who sent me to baptize with water told me, 'The man on whom you see the spirit come down and remain is he who will baptize with the Holy Spirit."* Maybe John said 'I would not have known him', because, like many others, he expected that the one to come would descend from the sky, the same way as Elijah ascended, described in 2Ki 2:11 as, *"As they* (Elijah and Elisha) *were walking along and talking together, suddenly a chariot of fire and horses of fire appeared and separated the two of them, and Elijah went up to heaven in a whirlwind."* And, when we turn to Isa 66:15-16, it is foretold, *"See, the LORD is coming with fire, and his chariots are like a whirlwind; he will bring down his anger with fury, and his rebuke with flames of fire. For with fire and with his sword the LORD will execute judgment upon all men, and many will be those slain by the LORD."*

When we read these words, we can believe that John indeed might have expected the arrival of the one for whom he was preparing the way to be a more glorious or a more supernatural event. He might have never imagined that the one everyone had been waiting for would appear in front of him with his face and his robe covered with dust from having walked too long without resting.

There was also the prophecy that is recorded in Mal 4:5 as, *"See, I will send you the prophet Elijah before the great and dreadful day of the LORD comes."* It seems that John did not understand that this verse was referring to him, because when he was asked if he was Elijah, he denied it: *"They asked him, 'Then who are you? Are you Elijah?' He said, 'I am not.' 'Are you the Prophet?' He answered, 'No.'"* (Jn 1:21) Nevertheless, Jesus asserted, *"And if you are willing to accept it, he is the Elijah who was to come."* (Mt 11:14) Regardless of his different convictions and beliefs John concluded: *"I have seen and I testify that this is the Son of God."* (Jn 1:34)

The story does not tell us where Jesus went after being baptized by the one who was called to prepare the way for Jesus. We do not know what John and his disciples did, as well as, whether Jesus and John spoke some more, however, we can presume that that night was unlike any other night for John and Jesus and that different decisions had to be made.

We do know that the next day John saw Jesus again, which meant that Jesus must have lodged close to John's camp. That meeting is described in Jn 1:35-36: *"The next day John was there again with two of his disciples. When he saw Jesus passing by he said, 'Look, the Lamb of God.'"*

THE LAMB OF GOD

The previous day John had recognized the lamb that was with Jesus as being the Lamb who takes away the sin of the world: *"Look, the Lamb of God, who takes away the sin of the world!"* (Jn 1:29) Now, let us look more closely at the lamb that was with Jesus, which many people believe was Jesus himself.

According to Jewish tradition a lamb, representing innocence and gentleness, was used as an offering for the forgiveness of sin, as for example it is said in Lv 5:6, *"... as a penalty for the sin he has committed, he must bring to the LORD a female lamb or goat from the flock as a sin offering; and the priest shall make atonement for him for his sin."* Therefore, when John testified to seeing the lamb, it means, in actuality, he was seeing a woman who had been restored to the state of innocence. At that time when John heard himself testifying that this lamb who was with Jesus would take away the sin of the world, he must have been extremely surprised to realize that through Jesus and the lamb the people could finally be entirely cleansed of their sins. (Jn 1:29)

Now the question is, after John had received this vision, did he humble himself to what he saw and heard, or did he re-question what he had experienced? Or, perhaps knowing both Jesus and the lamb from previous encounters, did he judge them as not following the religious traditions, or maybe even seek to have the lamb, which had been sanctified, for himself?

In the Bible, we find many references to lamb or to sheep. Jesus said on one occasion: *"I tell you the truth, the man who does not enter the sheep pen by the gate, but climbs in by some other way, is a thief and a robber. The man who enters by the gate is the shepherd of his sheep."* (Jn 10:1-2) And in Jn 10:7 Jesus said, *"I tell you the truth, I am the gate for the sheep. All who ever came before me were thieves and robbers, but the sheep did not listen to them. I am the gate; whoever enters through me will be saved. He will come in and go out, and find pasture. The thief comes only to steal and kill and destroy; I have come that they may have life, and have it to the full."* With these words Jesus clearly explained that he was the true shepherd of the sheep and at the same time that he was the gate to pass through for anyone who wanted to be saved.

Therefore regarding John, he not only needed to allow the sheep to go through the gate, who was Jesus, but also, he himself had to pass through Jesus in order to become a true shepherd of the sheep. And if he did not accept to 'enter the sheep pen by the gate' but tried to be a shepherd in his own way, he would be 'a thief and a robber.'

Since according to Mt 3:5, *"People went out to him* (John) *from Jerusalem and all Judea and the whole region of the Jordan,"* there must have been many women, or sheep, around John as well as many men, or goats. Now we might want to know if indeed John allowed the sheep to pass the gate, or in other words, to go to the true shepherd, or if he held on to his sheep. Maybe there was one sheep or lamb that was especially dear to John. Would he allow this one to be with Jesus as the true shepherd? If indeed John allowed the sheep that was closest to him to pass through Jesus as the gate, recognizing Jesus to be the true shepherd, this would be the offering that would make John pass through the gate as well. In doing so, he could become a true shepherd of sheep, like Jesus was. Now let us see what John did.

JOHN'S DISCIPLES BEGIN TO FOLLOW JESUS AND THE LAMB

When we look at the testimony that John as one of the greatest religious leaders of his time gave about Jesus, who was younger than him and less famous, we can say that John's way of witnessing was a great miracle by itself. Nevertheless, as we have indicated above, John was not only meant to testify about Jesus, but ultimately he himself had to humbly pass through Jesus as the gate to the Kingdom of Heaven. In other words, John needed to believe in Jesus and follow him, like some of John's disciples did after he introduced Jesus and the lamb to them: *"When he* (John) *saw Jesus passing by, he said, 'Look, the Lamb of God!' When the two disciples heard him say this, they followed Jesus."* (Jn 1:36-37) From this verse we can imagine that John's two disciples must have been very excited by Jesus and the lamb, and since they did not hesitate to abandon John, their present leader, they must have understood what Jesus came for. Regarding John, he might not have expected them to leave so suddenly.

Since there are no further details recorded, we do not know if there were more conversations between John and his disciples, who up to this moment had been respecting John as their guide. Nevertheless, we can assume that based on the revelations John had been receiving and his understanding of the secrets in the scriptures, his disciples must have been well educated. For this reason, when John was pointing out the 'lamb of God', they somehow must have understood the significance of what was taking place before their very own eyes. Jesus seemed to sense John's disciples' internal state when they approached him, asking them, *"What do you want?"* (Jn 1:38) The disciples then asked Jesus, *"'Rabbi (which means Teacher) where are you staying?' Jesus answered, 'Come and you will see.' So they went and saw where he was staying, and spent that day with him. It was about the tenth hour."* (Jn 1:39)

Jesus realized that John's disciples were in actuality questioning about whether they could follow him. Understanding their wish and their attraction to him, he told them to come, and so John's disciples excitedly spent the whole day with Jesus. Being so fascinated by Jesus' presence and the words he was speaking, they seemed to not notice the time passing. In their happiness to be with Jesus, the thought and the wish must have come to them from time to time that their leader John could be with them, listening to this teacher Jesus. They knew that many points that Jesus was talking about, John would like very much to hear. As they were captivated by Jesus' words, they began to understand much more deeply the truth that John had taught them and the prophecies he had given.

After this incredible meeting John's disciples went back to John's community. Full of excitement and hope they must have shared their experiences with everyone else. In Jn 1:41 it is stated, *"The first thing Andrew* (who was one of the two disciples) *did was to find his brother Simon and tell him, 'We have found the Messiah' (that is, the Christ)."* Deplorably, there is no record about the disciples going to John to report to him about their new hope, from which we can infer that somehow John might not have been so open to their discoveries and that there might have been some dilemma taking place within him.

After Andrew had testified to his brother that he had found the Messiah whom John had been prophesying about and that indeed this Messiah called Jesus was not like any other rabbi or any other person he had ever met, Andrew brought his brother to Jesus. It is recorded in Jn 1:42 that, *"Jesus looked at him and said, 'You are Simon son of John. You will be called Cephas' (which, when translated, is Peter)."*

Realizing that some of John's disciples welcomed and followed Jesus, we might ask, where was John? Where was this resilient individual who had been speaking in the wilderness all this time? Or, we might wonder, whether John was happy when he saw a group of his followers turning to Jesus? Was he happy that Jesus could be lifted up as the Messiah or did he harbor some different feelings about this new Messiah?

Looking through the Scriptures, after the initial encounter between Jesus and John, there are no further records about John accompanying Jesus, but only about John's disciples following the new rabbi. The reason could be that John did not share their views about Jesus and the lamb that was with him.

As we have discussed, in order for darkness to be removed from this world, the one who represents the side of darkness, who in this case was John, has to surrender to the one who represents the side of light, who was Jesus. In this sense, when John met Jesus at the Jordan River, John was confronted with a difficult test. Would he surrender to the lineage of light that came from Jesus and the lamb, or would John hold on to the lineage of darkness or the lineage of the viper that was within him?

And what would be the consequences for Israel and the rest of the world if John, who carried the hope for the darkness to be turned into light, refused to follow Jesus? Would everyone, like John, remain in darkness? Surely, after preaching about the coming of the great One, now John had to pass the test of not only mentally welcoming him but surrendering to him physically as well, by following Jesus and taking the same path as he.

BEING REBORN THROUGH A NEW GATE

Jesus repeatedly emphasized the importance of believing in him, of lifting him up and glorifying him. For example in Jn 3:3 Jesus explains to Nicodemus, a Pharisee, *"I tell you the truth, no one can see the kingdom of God unless he is born again."* And when Nicodemus was wondering how this could be possible when he had already been born, Jesus explained in more detail, *"I tell you the truth, no one can enter the kingdom of God unless he is born of water and the spirit. Flesh gives birth to flesh, but Spirit gives birth to spirit."* (Jn 3:5) With these words Jesus indicated that in order to receive the lineage of light we need to accept both the Son of God and the Holy Spirit who was with him, also referred to as the lamb.

In this regard, the great prophet John, after baptizing with water and testifying to the one who would come to baptize with the Holy Spirit, had also to accept to be reborn through the womb of the new mother, the same as Nicodemus and everyone else, now that the Holy Spirit had taken form. (Lk 3:22)

Nicodemus at first seemed to be shocked and puzzled by Jesus' answer of how to enter the kingdom of heaven. However, since we do not see him disagreeing with Jesus, he must have understood the meaning of being reborn after Jesus' more detailed explanation of how everyone, especially men, needed to welcome the woman with Jesus as the new mother. Maybe Nicodemus struggled because in his time men did not give the same value to women as to men. Still, the only way to enter the kingdom of God was to humble himself to the new womb as the gate that Jesus had created.

JESUS OR JOHN

After the encounter with Nicodemus we see Jesus and those who were with him returning to the Judean countryside where John was. Maybe Jesus still believed that the teacher John would decide to help those in darkness to accept him, Jesus, as the light. Until then, as Jesus sadly remarked, *"This is the verdict: Light has come into the world, but men loved the darkness instead of light, because their deeds were evil."* (Jn 3:19)

Once Jesus arrived to the countryside, he began to baptize those who came to him. Even though when John had first met Jesus he acknowledged that Jesus was the one who could baptize the people with the Holy Spirit and with fire, John continued to baptize with the water from the Jordan River: *"Now John was also baptizing at Aenon, near Salim, because there was plenty of water, and people were constantly coming to be baptized."* (Jn 3:23)

Some Israelites, seeing Jesus baptizing at one location and John baptizing at another, became confused: *"An argument developed between some of John's disciples and a certain Jew (certain Jews) over the matter of ceremonial washing. They came to John and said to him, 'Rabbi, that man who was with you on the other side of the Jordan—the one you testified about—look, he is baptizing, and everyone is going to him.'"* (Jn 3:25-26) People were questioning who was indeed removing sin, was it Jesus or was it John? And when they could not find an answer, they approached John himself to clarify this question. John answered, *"A man can receive only what is given him from heaven."* (Jn 3:27) Hearing such a reply, it seemed to his disciples that all of a sudden John's strength was gone and that John was no longer the fervent preacher they had known, the preacher who so powerfully spoke about repentance and baptism while proclaiming that someone would come after him more powerful than he. In Jn 3:28 John continued, *"You yourselves can testify that I said, 'I am not the Christ,'"* and when his disciples pressed him about what to do and asked if he himself decided to follow Jesus, he said after a few moments of silence, *"but I am sent ahead of him."*

Then John continued as recorded in Jn 3:29, *"The bride belongs to the bridegroom. The friend who attends the bridegroom waits and listens for him, and is full of joy when he hears the bridegroom's voice. That joy is mine, and it is now complete."* We might ask, was John indeed joyful? Was it easy for him to accept that he was not the bridegroom, that the women who had been looking up to him and coming to him to have their sins forgiven, now were turning to Jesus, who was on the other side of the Jordan? Furthermore, the day he had seen Jesus with the lamb and realized that the lamb had recognized her true bridegroom, was he indeed happy that God's will was being fulfilled? In reality it seemed that John was disoriented, struggling with what to do at this point in his life and leaving the choice of whom to follow to his disciples. It was at this time that he concluded that it was time for him to decrease: *"He must become greater; I must become less."* (Jn 3:30)

John's Decision

Then John added as recorded in Jn 3:31, *"The one who comes from above is above all; the one who is from the earth belongs to the earth, and speaks as one from the earth..."* When John spoke in this fashion, his disciples realized that although John acknowledged Jesus, he hadn't made up his mind to follow Jesus. They perceived that he would not take the road together with the Lord, which means, John would not humble himself before Jesus as the Lord, recognizing and following him as the true bridegroom. It seemed to them that instead John would remain in the wilderness until his death.

After this, John's disciples, who considered him as one of the greatest after the prophet Elijah, were struggling to continue to show their respect to John as their master. As they saw his hesitant attitude towards the one about whom he had said that he was not worthy to untie his sandals, they felt he was not true to his word. Subsequently, even though they still stayed with John, little by little his authority over them began to decrease.

They questioned what they should do. If they continued to follow John, they would die with him in the wilderness. If they changed their master, people would persecute them for not remaining loyal to John, who was still highly regarded by many. Nevertheless, they also felt by following John and choosing to take the road of decreasing or turning their back on Jesus, they would fail to fulfill God's will.

And so, after hearing what John had to say about the person on the other side of the river, there were many discussions between his disciples. John's disciples knew if John did not follow the one he had testified about, the people who had believed in John all this time would begin to question God's revelations through him. And, regarding the disciples' own destinies, if they, like John, had difficulty to humble themselves in front of Jesus as the bridegroom of the bride, they risked *"...God's wrath to remain on them."* (Jn 3:36) And of course, they would not be able to receive the life that Jesus and the lamb came to give and thus they would continue to remain in darkness, or sink even deeper into darkness.

THE BONDAGE OF SIN

Now let us look one more time at John's dilemma. Regardless of John's desire to have a relationship with God, and his subsequent search in the Scriptures and his ascetic lifestyle, no matter how much John strived to fulfill his longing for God, he was limited by his body that carried elements of sin, which caused a conflict between the wishes of his mind and the wishes of his body. Due to this reality John must have realized that no matter how long he preached, no matter how much he and the people repented and wanted to be cleansed of their sins, there was something within him and within them that would thwart whatever they wanted to accomplish on the road of purification.

And so, he and his followers could only keep the hope that their sin would be removed in its entirety one day. The rite of baptism, a ritual of cleansing by immersing oneself into water, was an external sign of that hope. While John baptized people with water, he would promise them that after him someone else would come who would baptize them with the water of life or with the Holy Spirit, (Mk 1:8) which would truly liberate them from their bondage of sin. John somehow knew that without this person he and everyone else would be obliged to live their lives as prisoners to their flesh and to die with sin still within them. This sin would always stop them from acting upon what they believed and wished to achieve, which means, they would be condemned to stay 'hypocrites', described in Isa 29:13 as, *"The Lord says, 'These people come near to me with their mouth and honor me with their lips, but their hearts are far from me...'"*

In order to no longer be accused of being hypocrites, John and all the people with him should have been eagerly awaiting the arrival of the anointed or divine one who could remove their hypocrisy, the one for whom John was called to prepare the way. Until the coming of this one, John and everyone with him needed to be on constant guard of their sin not taking over them. They were continuously reading the word of God and living a life of high discipline in order to stay on top of their sin, poignantly described by Jesus in Mt 18:7-9, *"Woe to the world because of the things that cause people to sin! Such things must come, but woe to the man through whom they come! If your hand or your foot causes you to sin, cut it off and throw it away. It is better for you to enter life maimed or crippled than to have two hands or two feet and be thrown into eternal fire. And if your eye causes you to sin, gouge it out and throw it away. It is better for you to enter life with one eye than to have two eyes and be thrown into the fire of hell."*

Therefore, even though John's standard was superior to the standard of the other religious leaders of his time, because of his inability to fully remove his sin, in particular the original sin, his fate was similar to everyone else. Like them, he would be unable to enter the Kingdom of Heaven, which was somehow close and yet far.

Once again we might question why John, who had been prepared so highly and at the same time was aware of the limitation of purification that he and his followers could achieve, made the wrong choice when meeting the person through whom everything could have been fulfilled.

THE REALITY OF THE HOLY SPIRIT

There is no record in the Bible that tells us what caused John to take the road opposite to the one God was hoping he would take, therefore people have not even realized that he took the wrong road and rather have believed that he was a saint. Actually, as we might have already discovered, it was not Jesus about whom John was struggling, but it was about the one who came with Jesus, called the lamb, the dove, or the Holy Spirit, that had become substance in the woman restored by Jesus. John himself announced the coming of the Holy Spirit when he declared in Mk 1:8, *"I baptize you with water, but he will baptize you with the Holy Spirit."* Nevertheless, when this became a reality, John must have forgotten his own prophecy.

Jesus referred to the Holy Spirit when he spoke to Nicodemus in Jn 3:5-7: *"I tell you the truth, no one can enter the kingdom of God unless he is born of water and the Spirit. Flesh gives birth to flesh, but the Spirit gives birth to spirit. You should not be surprised at my saying, 'You must be born again.'"* Furthermore, Jesus warned the people to not judge the Holy Spirit, told to us in Mt 12:32, *"Anyone who speaks a word against the Son of Man will be forgiven, but anyone who speaks against the Holy Spirit will not be forgiven, either in this age or in the age to come."*

From all these Bible verses we can deduce that Jesus could not give rebirth just by himself. People could receive life only by accepting Jesus and the woman who would come with him, who together would be their new parents. For this reason Jesus also said as stated in Mt 10:37, *"Anyone who loves his father or mother more than me is not worthy of me; anyone who loves his son or daughter more than me is not worthy of me."*

THE STORY OF CAIN AND ABEL

When God declared Jesus to be His favorite, we are reminded of the story of Cain and Abel in Ge 4:4: *"Abel brought fat portions from some of the firstborn of his flock,"* and *"The LORD looked with favor on Abel and his offering."* But, as portrayed in the next verse, in Ge 4:5, *"on Cain and his offering he did not look with favor. So Cain was very angry, and his face was downcast."* To help Cain overcome his feelings, God said to him, *"Why are you angry? Why is your face downcast? If you do what is right, will you not be accepted? But if you do not do what is right, sin is crouching at your door; it desires to have you, but you must master it."* (Ge 4:6-7)

In this sense, when God said to John the Baptist that He had accepted Jesus and his offering, symbolized by the lamb who came with Jesus, and that He, God, had given His blessing to him, calling Jesus His Beloved Son, we realize that John in regard to Jesus was in the same position as Cain towards Abel. God had not yet given His blessing to John, He had only endowed him with the mission of preparing the way for His son Jesus. Nevertheless, if, as Cain was meant to do, John followed what he heard within himself, which was to surrender to Jesus as God's Beloved, John would be able to master the sin within himself and God would be pleased with him as well. This means, John could also take the position of God's beloved. As John was confronted with what road to take, we surely can believe, as happened so many times in history whenever God had brought his Son, in that moment God must have been quite apprehensive about what John would do.

Based on his own experience of preaching to the people, John must have known that when someone could not accept

John's words, even to the point of becoming angry at him, it was because of the sin inside that person. Therefore, John should have realized that when he struggled to accept Jesus together with the lamb while God declared Jesus to be His Beloved Son, it must have been also because of the sin in him. To say it more clearly, the struggle caused by the appearance of the lamb exposed the sin John carried in his flesh. In fact, this was the sin that had been transmitted throughout history in all humankind. This mark can be traced back to the beginning of the creation of human beings when the woman whom God had meant to carry His holy lineage became corrupted, and instead became the vessel of the lineage of the serpent or the viper.

If John could have humbled himself to Jesus in that time, he truly would have fulfilled his mission of preparing the way for Jesus. If he had accepted Jesus and the lamb, he would have been the first one to remove the historical sin or the sin of the world, and thus he would have indeed become the greatest, as he was meant to be. (Mt 11:11)

But instead, when John met Jesus and the lamb and when the sin that had been dormant in him until that time suddenly became awakened, instead of using this situation to remove the sin that he still carried, John the Baptist pushed this chance away, saying about Jesus, *"He must become greater; I must become less."* (Jn 3:30) If, contrary to that, John had accepted to pass through the turmoil that he suddenly felt, his turmoil could have been transformed into a calmness that he had never been able to experience so far. Then John the

Baptist could have been legitimately recognized as the great-est preacher of all times and he would have been qualified to lead those who followed him, this time guiding them to be cleansed of their sin entirely.

It surely was God's hope that in the moment John met Jesus, John would use all the wisdom and all the experience he had gained to master the confusion of feelings that came to him in that moment. When John was not able to do that, these feelings festered within him and pushed aside all the knowledge and education he had received. Subsequently, when his disciples asked him whom they should follow, he as one of the most respected preachers of his time could just timidly conclude, *"The one who comes from above is above all; the one who is from the earth belongs to the earth, and speaks as one from the earth."* (Jn 3:31)

Besides creating confusion in his disciples, when uttering these words John must have deeply shocked God who had been preparing him for so long and yet, in this most decisive moment, He heard John speak as if he had received no prepa-ration at all. As well, witnessing this unexpected behavior from John must have been the worst experience that Jesus ever had. In the end, when John openly doubted Jesus, Jesus remarked about John as recorded in Mt 11:6, *"Blessed is the man who does not fall away on account of me."*

JESUS AS THE BRIDEGROOM

Regardless of all the confusion around Jesus and John, Je-sus was gaining more and more disciples: *"The Pharisees heard that Jesus was gaining and baptizing more disciples than John, al-though in fact it was not Jesus who baptized, but his disciples."* (Jn 4:1-2) The Pharisees, who accepted John but were suspicious of Jesus, observed Jesus' actions very closely. One day they sent some people to question Jesus, as related in Mk 2: 18: *"Now John's disciples and the Pharisees were fasting. Some people came and asked Jesus, 'How is it that John's disciples and the disciples of the Pharisees are fasting, but yours are not?'"* Since Jesus seemed to not follow the traditions, contrary to John who observed the religious rituals, the Pharisees obviously had become irritated by Jesus. He answered them as stated in Mk 2:19, *"How can the guests of the bridegroom fast while he is with them? They cannot, so long as they have him with them."* In this way, using the terminology of the bridegroom and the bride, as John had done when meeting Jesus, Jesus was basically saying to them, 'Why don't you enjoy to be with the bridegroom? How can you expect the bride and the guests to fast when he, the bridegroom, is here?' Then Jesus added: *"But the time will come when the bridegroom will be taken from them, and on that day they will fast"* (Mk 2:20), subtly warning the religious leaders that if they cannot accept what the bride and the guests do and if they stop them from fulfilling God's Will, the bridegroom will be taken away and from that day the bride, including all women and therefore also all men, will have to fast. This means that no one would be able to receive the life that Jesus as the bridegroom came to give. Since those who had come to interrogate him seemed to be puzzled by Jesus' answer, to help them better understand what he was saying Jesus used a parable: *"No one sews a patch of unshrunk cloth on an old garment. If he does, the new piece will pull away from the old, making the tear worse. And no one pours new wine into old wineskins. If he does, the wine will burst the skins, and both the wine and the wineskins will be ruined. No, he pours new wine into new wineskins."*(Mk 2:21-22) With these words Jesus was saying, in order to receive something new we have to accept to be transformed or to be 'reborn'. The 'old garments' or 'old wineskins' were an analogy of the people who questioned Jesus and the new wine that he wanted to give to them was the bride who already had been recreated by him.

JESUS' VISIT TO THE SYNAGOGUE IN NAZARETH

Since Jesus no longer had someone to prepare the way for him, he himself went throughout the country of Israel, in hope that the people would welcome him and believe in him. He also came to Nazareth, his hometown, where he visited the synagogue on the Sabbath as he had done many times when he was growing up: *"He went to Nazareth, where he had been brought up, and on the Sabbath day he went into the synagogue, as was his custom. And he stood up to read."* (Lk 4:16)

The rabbi of the synagogue offered the scroll of the prophet Isaiah to Jesus to read. Observing everyone for a short time, Jesus unrolled the scroll and looked through it. After a few minutes of silence Jesus addressed the people, who, eager to know what he would say, started to become impatient. He read to them the passage that is recorded in Lk 4:18-21: *"The Spirit of the Lord is on me, because he has anointed me to preach good news to the poor. He has sent me to proclaim freedom for the prisoners and recovery of sight for the blind, to re-lease the oppressed, to proclaim the year of the Lord's favor."* After hearing these words everyone became electrified. Lk 4:20-21 continues, *"Then he rolled up the scroll, gave it back to the rabbi and sat down. The eyes of everyone in the synagogue were fastened on him, and he began by saying to them, 'Today this scripture is fulfilled in your hearing.'"*

JESUS' BIRTH QUESTIONED

Listening to these words the people were stunned and amazed. Immense joy and hope started to fill the room: *"All spoke well of him and were amazed at the gracious words that came from his lips. 'Isn't this Joseph's son?' they asked."* (Lk 4:22) Suddenly, upon this question, the atmosphere changed dramatically. The light and expectation that had filled the room vanished and doubt, fear and darkness took its place. Maybe it was because the people remembered the gossip that was circling around at Jesus' birth, the rumors that indicated Jesus might not have been Joseph's son after all. As different memories came back to the people, instead of looking up they began to more and more look inward, to their darker side, and thus whatever they had experienced just a moment before began to disappear. Subsequently, the light that came to the people when they had listened to Jesus began to fade and darkness started to overtake them.

And so, as the audience turned their attention to Jesus' birth and upbringing that had created a lot of turmoil within and outside the walls of the synagogue, old rumors were revived and the people began to dismiss what Jesus had said and what they had felt. They closed themselves to whatever Jesus might have still wished to tell them. Perceiving the wall the people put up between them and Jesus, he remarked, *"I tell you the truth, no prophet is accepted in his hometown."* (Lk 4:24)

Jesus tried one more time to open their minds, asking them to recall the time of Elijah: *"I assure you there were many widows in Israel in Elijah's time, when the sky was shut for three and a half years and there was a severe famine throughout the land. Yet Elijah was not sent to any of them, but to a widow in Zarephath in the region of Sideon."* (Lk 4:25-26) With these words Jesus was warning the congregation in his hometown, if they, like the people in the time of Elijah, rejected him, calamities would befall them. They would have nothing to eat spiritually and the women would become widows since they would not be able to receive the bridegroom who was sent to them. Instead, Jesus would go to some other region where the inhabitants could welcome him more openly.

Feeling the people's unchanging resistance, Jesus referred to another event that took place in Elisah's time, *"And there were many in Israel with leprosy in the time of Elisha the prophet, yet not one of them was cleansed—only Naaman the Syrian."* (Lk 4:27) Jesus warned the people rejecting him that, as in Elisah's time, they not only would not see him perform miracles, like the cleansing of lepers, but they also would not be able to be cleansed of their internal leprosy, which means, cleansed of their sin.

Yet the people did not pay attention to Jesus' warning and rather became furious when they heard these words. Some of them did not just content themselves with harboring negative feelings against Jesus but resolved to physical action: *"They got up, drove him out of the town, and took him to the brow of the hill on which the town was built, in order to throw him down the cliff."* (Lk 4:29) And so, as the people brought back their memories of the so-called son of Joseph, we witness their extreme shift of feelings, from amazement to hatred.

As before, when John was struggling to accept Jesus, which in his case was because of Jesus' coming as the true bridegroom, now the people in Nazareth, Jesus' hometown, were struggling to accept him, this time because of his unconventional birth. Once again Jesus was left with no other choice but to go somewhere else, to a place where the people could be more open to him.

Jesus Encounters an Evil Spirit in Capernaum

After the hostile reception in Nazareth Jesus went to Capernaum, a town in Galilee, and on the Sabbath he began to teach the people. And people welcomed him there: *"They were amazed at this teaching, because his message had authority."* (Lk 4:32)

In the audience there was a rich man known to be possessed by an evil spirit. He shouted at Jesus, *"Ha! What do you want with us, Jesus of Nazareth? Have you come to destroy us? I know who you are—the Holy One of God!"* (Lk 4:34) Here, the spirit possessing the man testified to the identity of Jesus as God's son and at the same time was afraid of being destroyed by him, knowing that Jesus came to remove evil. We can also infer that Satan who is behind evil spirits seemed to be quite worried about Jesus' existence.

Having the power to judge evil, Jesus responded, *"'Be quiet! Come out of him!' Then the demon threw the man down before them all and came out without injuring him."* (Lk 4:35) When the people witnessed Jesus' authority over evil, *"All the people were amazed and said to each other, 'What is this teaching? With authority and power he gives orders to evil spirits and they come out!' And the news about him spread throughout the surrounding area."* (Lk 4:36-37) Even though the people were in awe of Jesus' power over evil, it seemed they did not fully understand who Jesus was. They looked at him more as an exorcist or a healer, which is even more clear when we study the events that followed.

JESUS AS A HEALER

After what had taken place in the synagogue, *"Jesus left the synagogue and went to the home of Simon. Now Simon's mother-in-law was suffering from a high fever, and they asked Jesus to help her."* (Lk 4:38) Giving in to their request Jesus removed the fever from her.

When the people heard about this, as recorded in Lk 4:40-41, *"... the people brought to Jesus all who had various kinds of sickness, and laying his hands on each one, he healed them. Moreover, demons came out of many people, shouting, 'You are the Son of God!' But he rebuked them and would not allow them to speak, because they knew he was the Christ."* When we see Jesus responding in this fashion to those who recognized him as the Christ, we can deduce that the people were not yet ready to understand his true identity.

When Jesus was abandoned by the one who was meant to prepare the people for him after John had decided to go his own way by becoming less (John 3:30), Jesus must have been trying to find a way to rebuild the lost preparation all by himself. His ultimate hope was to present himself to the people not just as the one who came to remove their bodily sicknesses but as the one who came to remove the internal sickness of their sin.

A Reed Swayed by the Wind

While Jesus was making straight the way on his own, we might ask what happened to John. When we look in Mk 1:14, it is written, *"After John was put in prison, Jesus went into Galilee, proclaiming the good news of God."* We find out that John was arrested and put in prison for publicly criticizing Herod's family; now, instead of John, Jesus was proclaiming, *"The time has come. The kingdom of God is near. Repent and believe the good news!"* (Mk 1:15)

While John was in prison, his disciples continued to come to him. At some point John told them to go and ask the one whom he had met at the Jordan River, *"Are you the one who was to come, or should we expect someone else?"* (Mt 11:3) When John's disciples presented this sad question that was so full of faithlessness and doubt in Jesus, he answered: *"Go back and report to John what you hear and see: The blind receive sight, the lame walk, those who have leprosy are cured, the deaf hear, the dead are raised, and the good news is preached to the poor. Blessed is the man who does not fall away on account of me."* (Mt 11:4-6)

Again we might question, what could make John, who had spent so many years in the wilderness looking for and living by the truth and who had received so many revelations from God, so disbelieving and unsure about all the experiences that had been given to him? Maybe John had forgotten that it was God and not John himself who made all these miracles possible. What else, after receiving the prophecy at the Jordan River that clearly testified to the purpose of Jesus' coming, could cause John to doubt whether Jesus indeed was the One?

What Jesus had proclaimed about those who would reject him now applied to John, who once had been the great prophet preparing the way for Jesus as the Lord but then had turned to self-centeredness and despair: *"This is the verdict: Light has come into the world, but men loved darkness instead of light because their deeds were evil. Everyone who does evil hates the light, and will not come into the light for fear that his deeds will be exposed. But whoever lives by the truth comes into the light, so that it may be seen plainly that what he has done has been done through God."* (Jn 3:19-21)

After John's disciples finally left, Jesus said about John to those who were with him: *"What did you go out into the desert to see? A reed swayed by the wind? If not, what did you go out to see? A man dressed in fine clothes? No, those who wear fine clothes are in kings' palaces."* (Mt 11:7-8) Emphasizing the tragedy of what had happened to John, Jesus then asked, *"Then what did you go out to see? A prophet? Yes, I tell you, and more than a prophet."* (Mt 7:9) Pausing as the people agreed with him, Jesus explained John's position more clearly by quoting Isaiah's prophecy, *"This is the one about whom it is written: 'I will send my messenger ahead of you, who will prepare your way before you.'"* (Mt 7:10)

Making his followers aware that indeed something was terribly wrong about John's attitude towards him, Jesus continued: *"I tell you the truth: Among those born of women there has not risen anyone greater than John the Baptist; yet he who is least in the kingdom of heaven is greater than he. From the days of John the Baptist until now, the kingdom of heaven has been forcefully advancing, and forceful men lay hold of it. For all the Prophets and the Law prophesied until John. And if you are willing to accept it, he is the Elijah who was to come."* (Mt 11:11-14) Upon hearing these words, which clearly indicated that John had come as one of the greatest but had sunk to the lowest place, the people who still believed John was a great prophet must have been shocked and perplexed, trying to grasp the magnitude of Jesus' words. Those who still followed John must have questioned if they should or should not abandon him. Some might have felt that John had betrayed their trust in him. Others, who already were loyal to Jesus, might have felt anger toward John for making the road difficult for Jesus instead of preparing the way for him.

After Jesus had opened the eyes of the people in regard to John and his words began to sink inside his audience, those who had followed John and had received his baptism that somehow had made them feel lighter for a short period of time but again had become weighted down by their sin, understood what Jesus was saying and agreed with him.

Jesus, who knew that his message would not be understood by everyone, said as stated in Mt 11:15, *"He who has ears, let him hear."* Not everyone would be able to accept that John did indeed come as the Elijah and thus as the last prophet of the book of the law to make straight the way for Jesus as the Lord. However, John did not fulfill his mission because in the end he could not accept Jesus and, in particular, the lamb who was with Jesus. Therefore, as a consequence of John's failure, or as Jesus said, as a consequence of 'forceful men laying hold of the kingdom of heaven', the people could not receive salvation and thus the kingdom of heaven could not come as predicted.

In Lk 7:31-32 Jesus is quoted as sadly remarking to the Pharisees, *"To what, then, can I compare the people of this generation? What are they like? They are like children sitting in the marketplace and calling out to each other: 'We played the flute for you, and you did not dance; we sang a dirge, and you did not cry.'"* With this analogy Jesus demonstrated to the Pharisees that because he did not do what they expected of him, they had a hard time to accept him.

Initially the Pharisees also had difficulties to respect John, when he decided to turn from them and the God they preached about and he went into the wilderness to find his own relationship with God. At that time they wanted to make the people believe that John was possessed by a demon, as recalled in Lk 7:33, *"For John the Baptist came neither eating bread nor drinking wine, and you say, 'He has a demon.'"* When seeing how many people came to John to be baptized, in fear of losing their congregations the Pharisees eventually came to acknowledge John. But now the religious leaders struggled with Jesus, who not only came as a prophet but as God's son: *"The Son of Man came eating and drinking, and you say, 'Here is a glutton and a drunkard, a friend of tax collectors and 'sinners.'"* (Lk 7:34)

In the end Jesus concluded as stated in Lk 7:35, *"But wisdom is proved right by all her children,"* indicating that by the fruits we know if the origin is good or bad. On another occasion Jesus used a similar analogy, noted in Lk 6:43-44, *"No good tree bears bad fruit, nor does a bad tree bear good fruit. Each tree is recognized by its own fruit. People do not pick figs from thorn bushes, or grapes from briers."*

Woman Anoints Jesus

One of the Pharisees was more open to Jesus. His name was Simon and in order for him to get to know Jesus better, he invited him to his house for dinner and Jesus accepted. While Simon and Jesus dined, and Simon used this opportunity to question Jesus on many different topics, a woman who was known as someone who did not obey the laws of Moses came to see Jesus: *"When a woman who had lived a sinful life in that town learned that Jesus was eating at the Pharisee's house, she brought an alabaster jar of perfume."* (Lk 7:37) Entering the room, the woman hesitated for a moment when she faced the judging eyes of the ones present, but then she approached Jesus and kneeled down in front of him. Emotions within her overflowed and the tears streamed down her cheeks as if her sorrow was heavy; she bowed her head to Jesus' feet, which she embraced and kissed. She then anointed Jesus' feet with the perfume that she had brought with her. This scene is described in Lk 7:38 as, *"and as she stood behind him at his feet weeping, she began to wet his feet with her tears. Then she wiped them with her hair, kissed them and poured perfume on them."*

This woman's display of feelings changed the ambiance in the room. To the ones who had a low regard for the woman, this moment seemed to be long and embarrassing, while others were moved by the woman's apparent adoration and love for Jesus and they began to feel tears and love for him and for her as well.

Simon, the host, was eagerly awaiting Jesus' response, thinking, *"If this man were a prophet, he would know who is touching him and what kind of woman she is—that she is a sinner."* (Lk 7:39) Jesus, who seemed to sense his thoughts, responded with a story: *"Simon, I have something to tell you. Two men owed money to a certain moneylender. One owed him five hundred denarii, and the other fifty. Neither of them had the money to pay him back, so he canceled the debts of both. Now which of them will love him more?"* (Lk 7:41-42) Simon answered as stated in Lk 7:43, *"I suppose the one who had the bigger debt canceled."* Jesus agreed with him and said, *"You did not give me a kiss, but this woman, from the time I entered, has not stopped kissing my feet. You did not put oil on my head, but she has poured perfume on my feet. Therefore, I tell you, her many sins have been forgiven—for she loved much. But he who has been forgiven little loves little."* (Lk 7:45-47) Then Jesus said to the woman, *"Your sins are forgiven, (...) Your faith has saved you; go in peace."* (Lk 7:48-50)

The story does not tell us if Jesus knew the woman before this meeting and if she was asking for forgiveness for something related to him or whether she was seeking Jesus' forgiveness for the wrongdoings in her life. But those present in the room who heard Jesus words began to wonder: *"Who is this who even forgives sins?"* (Lk 7:49)

After this event there is no further record of the Pharisee called Simon. Maybe in the moment he was impressed by the way Jesus had made him humble when he compared the attitude of this sinful woman with the attitude that he, Simon, as the host of the dinner had demonstrated towards Jesus. Nevertheless later on, like the prophet John, he might have re-questioned the incident that had occurred. As he was in the position of a religious leader, there were strict laws that separated him from women, especially the ones who were considered unclean. So why would this Jesus, who by many was regarded not only as a prophet but as God's son, allow these kinds of women to approach him so intimately? Could this man really be someone sent by God? Was this Jesus a sinner himself, who just knew how to speak well?

Since Jesus no longer had people in leadership positions to prepare the way for him and to testify about his holiness, it was easy for other people to doubt Jesus as well and to have all kinds of misperceptions about him. And many times, like John who had had a hard time to accept the lamb that came with Jesus, so also those who wanted to know who Jesus was, somehow perceiving that he was a special man, in the end dismissed him because of the women who were around him.

HISTORICAL CONSEQUENCES OF JOHN REJECTING JESUS

If John the Baptist had united with Jesus, John could have made the bridge between Jesus and the religious leaders who had come to highly respect John to the point they even considered he might be the Christ. And not only the priesthood, but even Herod, the King of Judea, had a high regard for John, expressed in Mk 6:20 as, *"... Herod feared John and protected him, knowing him to be a righteous and holy man. When Herod heard John, he was greatly puzzled; yet he liked to listen to him."* Therefore, if John the Baptist had used his talents and power to support what Jesus was doing and if John had testified about his experience of rebirth through Jesus and the lamb, he could have opened the eyes of the religious leaders as well as the political leadership to recognize Jesus. In this sense, John the Baptist could have helped the whole nation to unite with Jesus. For this reason we can say, John the Baptist carried the foundation of the whole nation for Jesus to be recognized or rejected as the Messiah.

Subsequently, when John did not turn to Jesus but continued on his own road, Jesus lost the entire foundation that John stood upon when Jesus came to him and which John was meant to hand to Jesus. This foundation had been accumulating long before John, described in Mt 1:17 as, *"Thus there were fourteen generations in all from Abraham to David, fourteen from David to the exile in Babylon, and fourteen from the exile to the Christ."* In order to remake this foundation that had been invaded due to John's doubt, Jesus had to begin witnessing on his own, starting from the bottom of society. This is the reason he reached out to the poor, to the sick and crippled, performing miracles among them, and to the outcasts of society, like the tax collectors and the prostitutes, as for example it is recorded in Mt 9:10, *"While Jesus was having dinner at Matthew's house, many tax collectors and 'sinners' came and ate with him and his disciples."*

Nevertheless, in spite of all the miracles Jesus performed and all the words he spoke, Jesus perceived that nobody seemed to understand his true mission, and he remarked in Jn 5:31-32, *"If I testify about myself, my testimony is not valid. There is another who testifies in my favor, and I know that his testimony about me is valid."* Further referring to John who once had testified about him, Jesus continued in Jn 5:33-35, *"You have sent to John and he has testified to the truth. Not that I accept human testimony; but I mention it that you may be saved. John was a lamp that burned and gave light, and you chose for a time to enjoy his light."*

Since John no longer gave light for Jesus' way, Jesus wanted to turn people's attention to God Himself, who had given many miracles through Jesus. Therefore he added, *"I have testimony weightier than that of John. For the very work that the Father has given me to finish, and which I am doing, testifies that the Father has sent me."* (Jn 5:36)

After being abandoned by John, Jesus knew it would be difficult to win over the religious leadership. Nevertheless, in hope that he could open their eyes to him and to what he wanted to give to them, he continued to address them, sometimes speaking to them directly, sometimes speaking to them in parables. In Jn 5:37-40 Jesus is recorded as saying to them, *"And the Father who sent me has himself testified concerning me. You have never heard his voice nor seen his form, nor does his word dwell in you, for you do not believe the one he sent. You diligently study the Scriptures because you think that by them you possess eternal life. These are the Scriptures that testify about me, yet you refuse to come to me to have life."* With these words Jesus sadly acknowledged that the religious leaders, who spent so much time studying every word of the Scriptures, as John did, could not humble themselves to the fact that the holy texts they had studied and the revelations they had received essentially testified about Jesus. It seemed that in the time of Moses the religious leadership demonstrated faithlessness towards Moses as well, because Jesus remarked in Jn 5:45-47, *"But do not think I will accuse you before the Father. Your accuser is Moses, on whom your hopes are set. If you believed Moses, you would believe me, for he wrote about me. But since you do not believe what he wrote, how are you going to believe what I say?"*

On the other hand, when someone who had secular power came to the religious leaders, they readily received this person and sought to gain his favor, which Jesus pointed out in Jn 5:43-44, *"I have come in my Father's name, and you do not accept me; but if someone else comes in his own name, you will accept him. How can you believe if you accept praise from one another, yet make no effort to obtain the praise that comes from the only God?"* In this way Jesus straightforwardly told the Pharisees that instead of looking to be accepted by God and welcoming the one He sent to them in order to finally build the kingdom that they had been preaching about, they were centered only on themselves. They were looking to be praised by people around them and were busy praising them in return. For this reason, making them aware that they indeed were not following God's will, like many before them, Jesus reproached them, *"You hypocrites! Isaiah was right when he prophesied about you: 'These people honor me with their lips, but their hearts are far from me. They worship me in vain; their teachings are but rules taught by men.'"* (Mt 15:7-9)

LAW OF THE SABBATH

Regardless of Jesus' efforts to win the priests, the darkness that had come upon John due to his failure also intensified the darkness around the other doctors of the law and priests. Nothing that Jesus said could make them see their hypocrisy. They continued to design different ways to accuse him. Once again they found an occasion, the account of which we find in Mt 12:1-2: *"At that time Jesus went through the grain fields on the Sabbath. His disciples were hungry and began to pick some heads of grain and eat them. When the Pharisees saw this, they said* to him, *'Look! Your disciples are doing what is unlawful on Sabbath.'* Jesus turned to the Pharisees and answered, *"... Have you never read what David did when he and his companions were hungry?"* (Mt 12:3) Pausing to give time to the priests to direct their minds to this particular part in the scriptures, Jesus continued: *"He* (David) *entered the house of God, and he and his companions ate the consecrated bread- which was not lawful for them to do, but only for the priests"* (Mt 12:4) Jesus further displayed his knowledge of the Scriptures by adding, *"Or haven't you read in the Law that on the Sabbath the priests in the temple desecrate the day and yet are innocent? I tell you that one greater than the temple is here. If you had known what these words mean, 'I desire mercy, not sacrifice,' you would not have condemned the innocent. For the Son of Man is Lord of the Sabbath."* (Mt 12:5-8) Through these words, which surely incited the Pharisees even more against him, Jesus was telling them that from God's view, he and his disciples were justified to eat grain on Sabbath, just as David and his companions had been. To make the Pharisees aware of how much out of context their accusations were and how little they needed in order to persecute and harass him, he pointed out that he wasn't even in the temple eating the consecrated bread – he and his disciples were just walking through a field, eating a few heads of grain. And even if they were in the temple, they would still have had the right to eat the bread because after all he as the Son of Man was above the law that had been given to the sinful people in order to constrain their sin. Sadly, instead of listening to Jesus, *"the Pharisees went out and began to plot with the Herodians how they might kill Jesus."* (Mk 3:6)

Who Were Jesus' Brothers and Mother?

Regardless of the opposition by the religious leaders, Jesus tirelessly continued to preach and to heal the people, in hope they would repent and receive him and accept the mission he came to fulfill in order to establish God's Kingdom on earth.

When his parents and brothers and sisters were told about Jesus going all over Israel and many people gathering around him looking to be healed by him and listening to his words, instead of supporting him, they tried to stop Jesus: *"..., they* (his parents) *went to take charge of him, for they said, 'He is out of his mind.'"* (Mk 3:21) Jesus realized that after being abandoned by John and the religious leaders, now his closest relatives also came against him.

It seemed his family had united with the priests, who accused him of being possessed by demons: *"And the teachers of the law who came down from Jerusalem said, 'He is possessed by Beelzebub! By the prince of demons he is driving out demons.'"* (Mt 3:22)

Disputing the Pharisee's claim, Jesus said to them, *"How can Satan drive out Satan? If a kingdom is divided against itself, that kingdom cannot stand. If a house is divided against itself, that house cannot stand. And if Satan opposes himself and is divided, he cannot stand; his end has come."* (Mk 3:23-26) And making them aware of how powerful he needed to be in order to be able to make Satan leave, he added: *"In fact, no one can enter a strong man's house and carry off his possessions unless he first ties up the strong man. Then he can rob his house."* (Mk 3:27)

When we turn to Lk 11:20, Jesus is portrayed as further demonstrating his authority in front of evil by saying to the Pharisees, *"But if I drive out demons by the finger of God, then the kingdom of God has come to you."* And in Lk 11:24-26 we can see Jesus using another example to make the Pharisees and the people with them understand the nature of evil and thus realize his supremacy over evil, explaining, *"When an evil spirit comes out of a man, it goes through arid places seeking rest and does not find it. Then it says, 'I will return to the house I left.' When it arrives, it finds the house swept clean and put in order. Then it goes and takes seven other spirits more wicked than itself, and they go in and live there. And the final condition of that man is worse than the first."*

Then he ended the conversation saying in Lk 11:23, *"He who is not with me is against me, and he who does not gather with me, scatters."* Based on this verse we can understand why, when finally his family arrived, Jesus did not want to see them. The encounter between Jesus and his family is described in Mt 12:46-49 in the following way: *"While Jesus was still talking to the crowd, his mother and brothers stood outside, wanting to speak to him. Someone told him, 'Your mother and brothers are standing outside, wanting to speak to you.' He replied to him, 'Who is my mother, and who are my brothers?' Pointing to his disciples, he said, 'Here are my mother and my brothers.'"* When Jesus was stopped in his speech by the person who announced the arrival of his family, Jesus did not turn to greet them but continued to speak to those gathered around him and declared them to be his family. We can thus realize that his disciples were more united with him and therefore closer to him than his own mother and brothers.

And, indeed, in Lk 8:21 Jesus more directly answered the person who made him aware of the presence of his family, *"My mother and brothers are those who hear God's word and put it into practice."* And, when we turn to Lk 11:27, where a woman who seemed to want to make Jesus more compassionate towards his mother saying, *"Blessed is the mother who gave you birth and nursed you,"* Jesus countered, *"Blessed rather are those who hear the word of God and obey it."* (Lk 11:28)

Witnessing the difficulties of those who have seen someone growing up to perceive this person from the viewpoint of God, we can understand the necessity for someone to testify to these people. Therefore once again John, who had been prepared for this task, was not only meant to announce Jesus' coming but he was meant to stay with Jesus, educating the people to see Jesus as God's son and not just as their friend, relative or member of their community with a dubious background.

KINGDOM NOT OF THIS WORLD

Since Jesus no longer had anyone who was respected by society standing together with him to assist in bringing about the judgment day and ushering in the Kingdom of Heaven, it was easy for people to revert to their old ways of life once Jesus left their town and went on his way to visit other places. This is the reason we see Jesus condemning the cities he had visited that did not recognize what he had done for them. Some of these cities were Korazin, Bethsaida and Capernaum: *"Then Jesus began to denounce the cities in which most of his miracles had been performed, because they did not repent. 'Woe to you, Korazin! Woe to you, Bethsaida! If the miracles that were performed in you had been performed in Tyre and Sidon, they would have repented long ago in sackcloth and ashes. But I tell you, it will be more bearable for Tyre and Sidon on the day of judgment than for you. And you, Capernaum, will you be lifted up to the skies? No, you will go down to the depths. If the miracles that were performed in you had been performed in Sodom, it would have remained to this day. But I tell you that it will be more bearable for Sodom on the day of judgment than for you.'"* (Mt 11:20-24)

Facing the hostility of the people around him, the lack of repentance and the lack of desire to build God's kingdom, to the point that he who had dedicated his life to realize God's ideal found himself being treated like a criminal, Jesus sadly remarked, *"My kingdom is not of this world. If it were, my servants would fight to prevent my arrest by the Jews. But now my kingdom is from another place."* (Jn 18:36)

At an earlier time when Jesus still had hope to establish the kingdom in the midst of the people he was sent to, or we can also say, when he was still looking to plant the seeds for the kingdom of heaven on earth, he described God's kingdom in Mk 4:26-27: *"This is what the kingdom of God is like. A man scatters seed on the ground. Night and day, whether he sleeps or gets up, the seed sprouts and grows, though he does not know how."* In Mk 4:30-32 Jesus used another parable to portray God's kingdom, saying, *"What shall we say the kingdom of God is like, or what parable shall we use to describe it? It is like a mustard seed, which is the smallest seed you plant in the ground. Yet when planted, it grows and becomes the largest of all garden plants, with such big branches that the birds of the air can perch in its shade."*

Nevertheless, after the mistake of John the Baptist, Jesus stated that, *"...the kingdom has been forcefully advancing and forceful men lay hold of it."* (Mt 11:12) Therefore, Jesus could not succeed in planting the seeds of the kingdom and becoming its king, which had been the purpose of his coming to this world.

At some point the Pharisees pressed Jesus with the question of when the kingdom of God would come. Jesus told them as written in Lk 17:20-21, *"The kingdom of God does not come with your careful observation, nor will people say, 'Here it is,' or 'There it is,' because the kingdom of God is within you."* Thereafter he remarked to his disciples as stated in Lk 17:22, *"The time is coming when you will long to see one of the days of the Son of Man, but you will not see it,"* indicating that there was no longer any chance for him to fulfill his mission.

JOHN THE BAPTIST BEHEADED

In Mt 14:3-5 we are told, *"Now Herod had arrested John and bound him and put him in prison because of Herodias, his brother Philip's wife, for John had been saying to him: 'It is not lawful for you to have her.' Herod wanted to kill John, but he was afraid of the*

people, because they considered him a prophet." However, when
Herod promised Herodias' daughter to give her whatever she
liked after she had danced for him, she requested the head
of John the Baptist and Herod had John beheaded in prison.
(Mt 14:10)

As soon as Jesus heard about the death of John, his hopes
that John the Baptist would recognize him and the lamb
finally vanished. Upon this devastating news, confirming
that he had indeed lost the one who was to prepare the way
for him, Jesus sought solitude, taking a boat away from the
shore to remove himself from his entourage. Nevertheless,
most of the people were unaware of the consequences of
John's death for Jesus, so they kept coming to be healed by
Jesus spiritually and physically. (Mt 14:13) Despite his sor-
rowful heart, not wanting to forsake his Father in Heaven,
Jesus decided to continue on his lonely, thorny road. And so,
coming back to shore, when Jesus saw a large crowd waiting
to be healed, he had compassion on them, and healed and
comforted the sick. (Mt 14:14)

JESUS BECOMING THE LORD OF SUFFERING

As Jesus continued to face faithlessness from those who had
been called by God to believe in him and to follow him and
he came to be heavily persecuted, the prophecy of Jesus coming as the glorious Lord could not be fulfilled.

In the book of the prophet Isaiah there are two prophecies regarding the Lord to come. One prophecy tells us of

him being welcomed and glorified by everyone:

"For to us a child is born, to us a son is given,
and the government will be on his shoulders.
And he will be called Wonderful Counselor, Mighty God,
Everlasting Father, Prince of Peace.
Of the increase of his government and peace there will be no end.
He will reign on David's throne and over his kingdom,
establishing and upholding it with justice and righteousness
from that time on and forever.
The zeal of the LORD Almighty will accomplish this." (Isa 9:6-7)

Another prophecy tells us that the coming Lord will be rejected and despised by everyone and will have to suffer many things:

"He was despised and rejected by men, a man of sorrows
and familiar with suffering.
Like one from whom men hide their faces he was despised,
and we esteemed him not.
Surely he took up our infirmities and carried our sorrows,
yet we considered him stricken by God, smitten by him, and
afflicted.
But he was pierced for our transgressions, he was crushed for
our iniquities;
the punishment that brought us peace was upon him,
and by his wounds we are healed." (Isa 53:3-5)

And so, because John and many other people who were in providential positions could not receive Jesus, the Son of God had to walk a path of sorrow. Eventually, Jesus as the one who was meant to bring the judgment together with the Holy Spirit, also referred to as the Spirit of Fire, could not fulfill the prophecy offered in Isa 4:4: *"The Lord will wash away the filth of the women of Zion; he will cleanse the bloodstains from Jerusalem by a spirit of judgment and a spirit of fire."* Alas, through these words we realize that because Jesus could not be received as the true bridegroom, the women were condemned to carry and pass on the lineage of corruption.

As well, instead of being recognized as the rightful King of the Jews and being crowned with a crown of gold with jewels, Jesus instead had to wear a crown of thorns, mocked as King of the Jews before being crucified: *"...* (They) *twisted together a crown of thorns and set it on his head. They put a staff in his right hand and knelt in front of him and mocked him. 'Hail, king of the Jews!' they said."* (Mt 27:29)

WE ARE GOD'S DWELLING PLACE ON EARTH

As we have been walking some of the journey of Jesus, we can only agree that the people who had been prepared to receive him were not simply to continue to uphold their faith in God after meeting Jesus, but they were to become his disciples, learn from him and eventually become perfect like him, which he asked his followers in Mt 5:48, *"Be perfect, therefore, as your heavenly Father is perfect."*

If those chosen to fulfill God's will, like John, could have found an attitude of humility in front of Jesus, they would have come to understand that everyone was created to resemble their Creator and that each individual was meant to be God's dwelling place on earth as Jesus was.

It Is Wise to Not Make a Statement

Accepting to see ourselves as historical people should help us to understand that it is wise to not make an absolute statement about someone or something being right or wrong. If we do not keep an open mind, we are in danger of judging what is not popular in the moment or judging something that is unknown to us. On the contrary, if we are careful with our attitude and choose not to judge, we are allowing the future to take a direction towards greater goodness.

Looking at John the Baptist's mistake, we might have wondered how it was possible that a person who had led such an exemplary and humble life in the desert could make a mistake with such devastating consequences. How was it possible for John who was living an ascetic life for so many years, to choose in the end to not humble himself in front of the one who was indeed greater than him?

As to our lives, we need to be sure to not let pride remain in us, therefore we should choose a humble attitude towards every situation and every person we happen to meet. This attitude will especially prepare us to meet the One who comes as the rock or the Christ. (1Co 10:4) And if indeed we have a chance to meet Christ or the Messiah, and if we can be humble in front of him, we will be able to make the transition from the stage of faith to the stage of love. This means, by being careful not to judge others or events that we are simply not able to fully understand in the moment, we can develop a beautiful character that will allow us to welcome the one who can take us from the stage of believing in the word to the stage where God's love can come to us.

CAIN AND ABEL STORY REPEATED IN JESUS' TIME

Here I would like to bring back the story of Cain and Abel, described in Genesis. We compared them earlier to John the Baptist and Jesus respectively: John the Baptist was in the position of Cain and Jesus was in the position of Abel, since he was loved by God more than anyone in his time. If Cain accepted Abel and humbled himself in front of him instead of killing him, Cain could have learned from Abel to make an offering that would be also pleasing to God. Then Cain could have been loved by God as well.

Moreover, Cain's unity with Abel as God's Beloved would have allowed Abel or Jesus to become the Messiah so that the people, too, could reach the realm of God's love. If John, who was highly respected by the people of his time, had united with Jesus who came with the lamb, Jesus together with the lamb could have taken the position of Messiah. Then, following John, the people would have been able to pass through the gate to the Kingdom of Heaven.

If John had accepted Jesus, his victory would have reversed the mistake of Cain who killed Abel. Then instead of a history of crime, goodness could have advanced in the world. In this sense, the choice that John made not only affected his own destiny, but it also affected the direction of evil or good-ness on a worldwide level.

Judging the Holy Spirit

As a religious person John the Baptist knew that goodness, in word or action, could not come from any human being who did not live a life of goodness: *"The good man brings good things out of the good stored up in him, and the evil man brings evil things out of the evil stored up in him."* (Mt 12:35) He also chastised the Pharisees and Sadducees: *"... You brood of vipers! Who warned you to flee from the coming wrath? Produce fruit in keeping with repentance. And do not begin to say to yourselves, 'We have Abraham as our father.' For I can tell you out of these stones God can raise up children for Abraham."* (Lk 3:7-8)

It seems some judgments are more detrimental than oth-ers to the person who pronounces the judgment, which we can see from Jesus' words when he warned those around him about the mistake of speaking against him, and even worse than that, speaking against the Holy Spirit: *"Anyone who speaks a word against the Son of Man will be forgiven, but anyone who speaks against the Holy Spirit will not be forgiven, either in this age or in the age to come."* (Mt 12:32)

Indeed John should have been more careful not to judge the woman who stood with Jesus as the physical representa-tion of the Holy Spirit. Unfortunately, despite John's visions and prophecies, it seems that John had difficulties to accept the Holy Spirit who came with Jesus, even though officially John admitted that Jesus came as the bridegroom and that the bride belonged to Jesus and not to himself, recorded in Jn 3:29 as, *"The bride belongs to the bridegroom. The friend who attends the bridegroom waits and listens for him, and is full of joy when he hears the bridegroom's voice. That joy is mine, and is now complete."* Once John could no longer keep this view, he began to struggle highly, to the point he began to question if Jesus indeed was the one everyone had been waiting for, related to us in Lk 7:20 as, *"When the men* (John's disciples) *came to Jesus, they said, 'John the Baptist sent us to you to ask, "Are you the one who was to come, or should we expect someone else?"'*

In this regard, we who live in a different time of history can learn from the mistake of John the Baptist that it is wise to be patient and to allow different events to take form or 'produce fruits' before we make a statement about them or judge them to not be in accord with our beliefs and traditions. For example, instead of rejecting a new idea or event we are faced with, it is better to simply recognize it as being different. Training ourselves to have this kind of attitude, we should be able to do the right thing at the time when we are called to do so.

As well, we need to know that God is always trying to present us with something new, something that we have never known or experienced before in order to elevate our character and to grow His goodness in us. Therefore, God might ask us to do something that we never did or do something that is not in accordance with our beliefs.

Indeed, God's ultimate goal for John the Baptist was not only to be the one to prepare the way for the Lord, but to continue in his growth until he became one in heart with the Lord. This means, ultimately God wanted John to be perfect as his heavenly Father is perfect. In this regard, John was not only meant to testify about Jesus but eventually he was meant to become Jesus' greatest disciple. If he had welcomed Jesus and the Holy Spirit and received the love coming from them he would have been able to be cleansed from the blood of the viper and to carry the lineage of life.

DUALITY IN LIFE

Another important point to keep in mind is that, according to the law of God, in order for anything to have life, to grow and to receive love, there needs to be duality or harmony. If we begin to reject something or someone, we promote another kind of law that opposes the God of love.

The law of duality begins with simple everyday situations. For example, if someone smiles to us, to practice the law of duality we simply need to smile back to that person. If someone gives us a hand to greet us, we want to return the handshake; and if someone asks for help it is humble to respond and to help. By practicing this kind of attitude every day in all kinds of situations we prepare ourselves to one day welcome the chosen one who is qualified to bring us to the dwelling place of God's love. However, if we reject the law of duality, we will not be able to recognize God's chosen one who can show to us how to fulfill our destiny of becoming the children of God.

If we humbly accept any kind of circumstances, as John must have learned in the beginning of his life of faith, we will often meet limitations of patience and faith. Nevertheless, if we decide to take the path of humility, even when someone harshly makes a request from us, instead of perceiving this person's action as rude or evil, we will see it as helping us to reach a place of even greater humility.

With this understanding we might assume that John, who seemed to have trained himself well internally and externally, should have known that the one who is behind the nature of rejection, who is Satan, would do anything to discourage him from responding to Jesus who challenged John's faith and obedience. John should have been aware that by doubting and eventually rejecting his cousin Jesus and the Holy Spirit he was accomplishing the will of Satan instead of fulfilling the Will of God.

Knowing the nature of evil, which is the nature against duality, especially against duality with the Son of God, Jesus sought to prepare his disciples to have faith and obedience in any kind of situation, saying to them as recorded in Lk 6:30-31, *"Give to everyone who asks you, and if anyone takes what belongs to you, do not demand it back. Do to others as you would have them do to you."* On another occasion Jesus taught his followers as recorded in Lk 6:37-38, *"Do not judge, and you will not be judged. Do not condemn, and you will not be condemned. Forgive, and you will be forgiven. Give, and it will be given to you. A good measure, pressed down, shaken together and running over, will be poured into your lap. For with the measure you use, it will be measured to you."*

If those who listened to him accepted this training, they would be able to develop a character of goodness, which would make them qualified to welcome and to receive the love of the one whom God called His Beloved Son. (Mt 3:17)

Today's prevailing opinion among religious people is that John was a great person who fulfilled God's will. However, in view of what we discussed earlier, we can see that such a statement is far from the truth.

Let us take a moment to look at John's attitude when he approached the people who were less prepared than him, whether he sought to make duality with them and lift them to a higher place, and whether at the same time he showed humility in front of all the situations he encountered.

Unfortunately there are not too many records in the Bible referring to John's relationships with the people. We are told that he was baptizing them and asking them to repent in preparation to meet the one who would be greater than him. He also taught his followers in Lk 3:10-14: *"'The man with two tunics should share with him who has none, and the one who has food should do the same.' Tax collectors also came to be baptized. 'Teacher,' they asked, 'what should we do?"' Don't collect any more than you are required to,' he told them. Then some soldiers asked him, 'And what should we do?' He replied, 'Do not extort money and don't accuse people falsely—be content with your pay.'"* From these words we can deduce that John had some understanding of following the law of duality and humility.

Jesus not only taught the law of duality but he completely lived it as well. He understood deeply that ultimately God's will was to make His love dwell on earth. For this reason people perceived Jesus not only as a teacher but they also felt love and healing coming from him.

To demonstrate that Jesus' ultimate goal was to give life or love to the people, let us turn to the Gospel of John. There we can read about a woman who met Jesus at the well of Jacob where Jesus spoke to her about the living water, which means, the love that he would be able to give to her, whereupon the woman wondered, *"Are you greater than our father Jacob, who gave us the well and drank from it himself, as did also his sons and his flocks and herds?"* (Jn 4:12) Jesus answered to her, *"Everyone who drinks this water will be thirsty again, but whoever drinks the water I give him will never thirst. Indeed, the water I give him will become in him a spring of water welling up to eternal life."* (Jn 4:13-14)

Regarding John, besides preaching about baptism and repentance, and giving guidance to his followers, we also see him confronting King Herod for having broken the law of religion, noted in Mk 6:18 as, *"For John had been saying to Herod, 'It is not lawful for you to have your brother's wife.'"* John thus was a righteous person who did not fear death. In order for John to accuse Herod of not following the law, John must have believed himself to be quite powerful and without blame and more than just someone who was humbly preparing the way of someone greater than him.

Maybe John forgot that what we do to others, it will be done to us, or that if we judge, judgment will come to us, and especially if we accuse something or someone who is not blamable, darkness and confusion will overtake us. Maybe John had forgotten that it was God who had raised him and he came to believe whatever he had achieved was due to his own efforts. This might be the reason that he began to put himself above others.

Maybe it was John's self-righteousness that blinded him to such a degree that when he finally met Jesus, the one whose sandals he was not worthy to untie, and after initially perceiving Jesus' greatness, John later shifted his position and saw himself equal to Jesus, or maybe greater or more righteous than he. As we know there are stories recorded in the Bible telling us that many times Jesus was accused by the Pharisees of not following the religious laws. For the same reason, even though in the beginning John perceived that Jesus came to bring judgment to him, John might have begun to judge Jesus instead. And, not having practiced the law of duality and humility, John eventually was unable to respond to Jesus and to follow him, contrary to some of his own disciples.

And so, according to God's law – 'the measure you use will be measured to you' – when John not only began to judge other sinners but also began to judge the one who had no sin, who was Jesus with the lamb, then John's destiny began to change. When he no longer followed God's principles, God could no longer protect him. Therefore even though, *"Herod feared John and protected him, knowing him to be a righteous and holy man....,"* (Mk 6:20) Herod eventually put John in prison, stated in Mk 6:17 as, *"For Herod himself had given orders to have John arrested, and he had him bound and put in prison. He did this because of Herodias, his brother Philip's wife, whom he had married."* And, as we know, after being imprisoned John was beheaded upon Herod's order. Regardless of the circumstances that led to this order, John's life ended in this way because he could not respond to Jesus and the Holy Spirit, finally re-questioning if Jesus really was the one.

Learning from what happened to John the Baptist, it would be wise to train our mind and our flesh to follow the law of duality by 'doing to others as we would have them do to us', which means, to respect them as we wish to be respected and serve them as we wish to be served. In this way we will prepare ourselves to receive the One God sends to us and to at last pass through the gate to God's kingdom, which seems to be especially hard if we are endowed with many talents and gifts. Knowing this difficulty, Jesus said as written in Mt 19:23, *"I tell you the truth, it is hard for a rich man to enter the kingdom of heaven. Again I tell you, it is easier for a camel to go through the eye of the needle than for a rich man to enter the kingdom of God."*

GOD'S WILL IS LIKE A SPHERE

According to Lk 1:5-6, John came from a special family: *"In the time of Herod king of Judea there was a priest named Zechariah, who belonged to the priestly division of Abijah; his wife Elizabeth was also a descendant of Aaron. Both of them were upright in the sight of God, observing all the Lord's commandments and regulations blamelessly."*

Knowing that John came from a long line of priests who had been serving the temple, we can assume that he was well-educated in the knowledge of religion. Therefore he must have realized that God's providential will is like a sphere, every so often coming to the same turning point. He must have understood that every time the people did not heed the warnings of the prophets whom God had sent and many times even killed God's messengers and thus prevented God's will from being achieved, the entire population had to undergo a new round of suffering. One thing that we can say for sure is that John knew that he was the prophet who was preparing the way for God's will or God's kingdom to be fulfilled.

God educated John and sent him to the Israelites in hope that the mistakes made in the time of Elijah would not be repeated. If John had fulfilled this call, the people would not have had to continue to undergo hardships under Satan, but God's kingdom could finally be built among them and they could live in God's love. This means, John was called to stop history from repeating itself through another round. If he had obeyed God's command and humbled himself to become Jesus' follower, he would indeed have made the way straight for Jesus and stopped the historical cycle of suffering.

To fail in the moment that had been most anticipated by God, John must have become careless in preparing himself in accordance with the law of duality. In order to be ready to accomplish his mission John should have been diligent every moment of his life. For example, he should have looked upon every event that came to him in his daily life as a chance to elevate himself and thus he should have welcomed every challenge. Based on being sincere with what he heard in his conscience and observing his relationship with God, he should have been aware that everything he rejected made him go down in his spiritual development. He should have known that it was not only important for him to increase his intellectual understanding or to challenge his physical stamina, but most importantly he needed to be strict with his attitude towards welcoming everything that came to him in order to develop his nature of goodness and increase his humility. In this sense, the more John advanced in his life of faith, the more careful he needed to be and the less judgment he should have pronounced. He needed to be extra cautious to listen to God's voice inside of him, so that he would never be tempted to make a mistake, especially in a moment that was crucial, like the moment that would determine if history would advance or repeat itself.

When John failed to make the right choice, he indeed decreased. However, it was not his pride that decreased. Instead, John became confused and darkness began to overtake him, to the point that Jesus sadly remarked about John as written in Mt 11:11, *"I tell you the truth: Among those born of women there has not risen anyone greater than John the Baptist; yet he who is least in the kingdom of heaven is greater than he."* And, witnessing John's journey, we might be reminded of the prophecy that Simeon gave when he saw Jesus as a baby: *"Then Simeon blessed them and said to Mary, his mother: 'This child is destined to cause the falling and rising of many in Israel, and to be a sign that will be spoken against.'"* (Lk 2:34)

AN ANSWER TO OUR PRAYER

From another perspective we can say that the coming of Jesus was the answer to John's prayer. Yet, after many years of preaching repentance and preparing the people for the one who could indeed liberate them from their sin by baptizing them not only with water but with the Holy Spirit, when the long-awaited time finally came but in a different way than he had imagined, John ended up rejecting it. Actually, God answered John's prayer several times, helping him through revelations and visions to be able to surrender to Jesus and the one who was with him. (Jn 1:28, 32, 36)

When John refused to receive the answer to what he had been preparing and praying for all his life, his choice led to a series of events. His life came to a sudden and brutal end and Jesus, as the one who came to remove the sin of the world, had to rebuild the foundation that had been lost by trying to find a way for people to believe in him. This task became more and more difficult since many believers had become confused after they saw Jesus and John going separate ways.

Moreover, those who had been waiting for the liberation from their sin had to continue to wait and were even more heavily imprisoned by their sin due to John's failure that brought darkness not only to himself but to all the nation. Subsequently, all of God's efforts to raise up John the Baptist and through him the people of Israel were in vain. Instead God had to watch the people abandon His Beloved Son Jesus and once again see His Son going the road of suffering.

If we use an analogy for John's situation, it is like someone who is sick, even though John was less sick than others, rejecting the doctor he has been waiting for to bring a cure. As a consequence, the person's sickness cannot be cured and it can only grow worse since there might be no other remedy to contain and heal the sickness. In this case, the 'sickness' was carried from generation to generation through the sin-stained blood of the viper. With the rejection of God's Will, the characteristics that had been transmitted through this blood were reinforced, bringing John closer to the origin of the contamination that he had been working so hard to leave behind. As well, when John as the leader of many people chose to decrease before Jesus instead of accepting to be healed or saved by him, it was inevitable that John's followers who trusted him would do the same. They also turned their backs on Jesus and eventually Jesus came to be accused to be a false doctor or a charlatan: *"And the teachers of the law who came down from Jerusalem said, 'He is possessed by Beelzebub! By the prince of demons he is driving out demons.'"* (Mk 3:22) When John the Baptist and other religious leaders turned against Jesus, some of them quite violently, Jesus eventually advised those who followed him, *"Every plant that my heavenly Father has not planted will be pulled up by the roots. Leave them; they are blind guides. If a blind man leads a blind man, both will fall into a pit."* (Mt 15:13-14)

Therefore, if we want to learn from the mistake of John the Baptist, we need to be careful to not reject the answer to our prayer in whatever form it may come and be grateful when someone offers us the cure for our sickness. Let's keep in mind that most of the time the remedy is different from what we would expect and it is therefore not easy to accept.

Recognizing the Grace of God

Another important lesson we can learn from the life of John the Baptist is that if we as individuals or as a group begin to prosper internally as well as externally, it is due to the grace of God, even though at times we might receive persecution from others.

Maybe, after initially being grateful to God for everything, John became used to the grace he received and considered all the understanding that was given to him and all the recognition he received from the people to be his own achievement. Therefore, disregarding the blessings bestowed on him by God, John found himself one day removed from God's protection and, instead of light and hope, darkness and despair were surrounding him.

In this sense, if John were less concerned about what was right or wrong and more sensitive to the benevolence of God, he surely would have recognized that whatever he was able to accomplish was because God was helping him, hoping that John would do something great in the future. It was for this reason that God continued to bless him, even though He might not always have been pleased with John's attitude. If John had this awareness, he would have been very careful about the manner in which he was conducting himself. He would have spent less time chastising people and more time worried about maintaining his connection with God and trying to understand God's wish for him.

If indeed John had acted with such care in regard to God and the people, he also would have been very careful about the way he acted towards Jesus when he met him. He would have sought God's guidance, asking God about the plans He had for him and Jesus. Then he might have realized that it would be good to abandon what the Scriptures or his own wisdom advocated and instead to be open to what Jesus had to say and to what Jesus did. For this reason Jesus taught in Jn 5:24-25, *"I tell you the truth, whoever hears my word and believes him who sent me has eternal life and will not be condemned; he has crossed over from death to life. I tell you the truth, a time is coming and has now come when the dead will hear the voice of the Son of God and those who hear will live."* In Jn 5:39-40 Jesus is speaking to the priests the words that he might have wanted to say to John as well: *"You diligently study the Scriptures because you think that by them you posses eternal life. These are the Scriptures that testify about me, yet you refuse to come to me to have life."*

It seems that John did not seek God's guidance but relied on his present understanding and judgment. Therefore he could not open himself to what God wanted to give. In order to do that, he needed to abandon all his knowledge and status and have the attitude of a child in front of God and Jesus: *"... Let the little children come to me, and do not hinder them, for the kingdom of God belongs to such as these. I tell you the truth, anyone who will not receive the kingdom of God like a little child will never enter it."* (Mk 10:14-15)

Having the heart of a child is the attitude that allows us to receive the love of God, which will nourish us and enable us to claim our place in God's kingdom. For this reason, if we want to be like a child in front of God or in front of the one God sends to us, whether we are prophets, preachers, teachers or simple believers, we need to recognize God's grace in everything. We can never become too confident about what we have achieved or what we know, but we need to always be open to learn something new and withhold our judgment.

As we follow the rise and downfall of John the Baptist, we might remember other figures or groups that were prominent at certain times in history but then ended up being forgotten or were faced with a sudden and violent end. Maybe in their times there was also a son of God who had been rejected, by them or someone else. Indeed, it is important to realize that the sudden prosperity of a person or of a group of people is due to God's grace, and the sudden misery or wars that follow are due to the denial of God's grace.

Accordingly, learning from the mistakes of those before us, it would be wise to have an attitude of humility in everything, emphasized by Jesus in Mt 18:3-4 as, *"I tell you the truth, unless you change and become like little children, you will never enter the kingdom of heaven. Therefore, whoever humbles himself like this child is the greatest in the kingdom of heaven."* If we choose to not take this kind of attitude, we are in danger of God's grace being removed from us: *"For whoever exalts himself will be humbled ."* (Mt 23:12)

Furthermore, even though there is no clear record in the Holy Book about what God's will is and many things are revealed to us in symbols, if indeed we display an attitude of humbleness and openness, we might receive the insights to understand God's will through these symbols, as Jesus declared to his disciples in Lk 8:10: *"The knowledge of the secrets of the kingdom of God has been given to you, but to others I speak in parables, so that, though seeing, they may not see; though hearing, they may not understand."* Or, as stated in Mt 13:11-15, *"The knowledge of the secrets of the kingdom of heaven has been given to you, but not to them. Whoever has will be given more, and he will have an abundance. Whoever does not have, even what he has will be taken from him. This is why I speak to them in parables: 'Though seeing, they do not see; though hearing, they do not hear or understand.' In them is fulfilled the prophecy of Isaiah: 'You will be ever hearing but never understanding; you will be ever seeing but never perceiving. For this people's heart has become calloused; they hardly hear with their ears, and they have closed their eyes. Otherwise they might see with their eyes, hear with their ears, understand with their hearts and turn, and I would heal them.'"*

FOLLOW THE VOICE INSIDE US

When we are faced with a choice, no one can make it for us, because we are the only ones who will be held responsible. As well, in that moment we cannot just rely on our previous knowledge and experience, because the choice is taking place in the present within present circumstances. Therefore, no matter how well he knew the Holy Scrolls, when John was asked to make a choice after meeting Jesus at the Jordan River, in that very moment it was not his knowledge that was most important, but his humbleness towards the situation presented to him.

John must have demonstrated some degree of humbleness, because after baptizing Jesus he was able to hear God's voice testifying to Jesus. (Mt 3:17) Nevertheless, after this initial humility, John must not have been able to keep this attitude, therefore he decided against joining Jesus and chose to walk his own way, which brought about his decline and eventually his death.

In the same way, how sincere are we to listen to and to follow the voice inside of us? Our obedience to that voice on a daily basis will help us to make the right choice when God sends His Son to us. This is the reason Jesus said, *"Not everyone who says to me, 'Lord, Lord,' will enter the kingdom of heaven, but only he who does the will of my Father who is in heaven."* (Mt 7:21)

The same as John was given a choice when he met Jesus, so also each of John's followers was asked to make a choice. Whatever decision they made was theirs alone and was what they would be held responsible for. They were not meant to just blindly follow John, and if they did, eventually realizing that this was the wrong choice, they could not accuse John, because only they were responsible for whatever they had done. It seems that many of John's followers just followed him blindly, like sheep that follow the leading sheep, even if it decides to jump off a cliff.

We are only told about a few of John's disciples following their conscience and their heart when John testified in Jn 1:36 as Jesus was passing, *"Look the Lamb of God."* Right in that moment two disciples changed their loyalty from John to Jesus, even though John continued on his own way. This means, when John introduced Jesus and the lamb to these two disciples, they understood the significance of what he was saying, that the moment they had been promised and were waiting for had finally arrived.

Besides this event recorded in one of the Gospels, many of John's other disciples must have heard or recalled John's testimony about Jesus as well. We should then ask the question, what they did they do after that? Did they follow their conscience or push away what they heard? Maybe many of them did not hear their conscience because they did not turn to God and ask Him what His will was for them. And so, they made the same mistake as John the Baptist did, continuing their lives as if nothing had happened, not being aware that in doing so they would lose all the foundation of faith and obedience they had built until this point.

Regarding ourselves, we need to always be open to what God or our conscience is telling us, so that in a decisive moment that not only determines our own fate but the fate of history, we can perceive God's message and make a choice in accordance with His will and His providence. To demonstrate the tragedy of people being caught in their daily lives and in their own perceptions, Jesus gave the parable of the wedding banquet in Mt 22:2-5: *"The kingdom of heaven is like a king who prepared a wedding banquet for his son. He sent his servants to those who had been invited to the banquet to tell them to come, but they refused to come. Then he sent some more servants and said, 'Tell those who have been invited that I have prepared my dinner: My oxen and fattened cattle have been butchered, and everything is ready. Come to the wedding banquet.' But they paid no attention and went off—one to his field, another to his business."*

We might believe that when God speaks to us it is about something that is extraordinary and otherworldly, but most of the time it is about something connected to our physical lives and/or present circumstances. John would not have been able to hear God witnessing to him about Jesus and seen a vision of a dove if Jesus had not physically appeared in front of him and if there was no one with Jesus who represented the dove. As well, John could hear God speaking to him, not because he himself was special, but because a special person had come to him.

Tragically, the Holy Book contains only a few descriptions of the appearance of God's Beloved and the impact he had on those who saw him, because the words, visions and feelings that people received when meeting the Son of God were given to them in private and they did not openly verbalize them. In addition, God speaks to people in ways that only they can understand; He speaks to them according to their spiritual level and their education.

Therefore, it is so important to take seriously the words we hear individually in the present moment and not just trust in the knowledge we have accumulated or the knowledge someone else offers to us. Learning from John's mistake and understanding the consequences of the choices we make, if in our lifetime we have the incredible chance to meet the Son of God, we need to believe in what we hear from him and inside of us, even though it might seem quite unusual or unconventional to us. If we can do so, we will allow the Son of God to lead us to the place where he and his Father dwell: *"As the*

Father has loved me, so have I loved you. Now remain in my love. If you obey my commands, you will remain in my love, just as I have obeyed my Father's commands and remain in his love. I have told you this so that my joy may be in you and that your joy may be complete." (Jn 15:9-11) Therefore, if we can make the right choice and welcome the Son of God who is said to return in our lifetime, this will finally fulfill the prophecy stated in Rev 22:5: *"There will be no more night. They will not need the light of a lamp or the light of the sun, for the Lord God will give them light. And they will reign for ever and ever."*

In this sense, instead of the cycles of darkness and light being repeated, we will be able to see history taking a direction towards increasing goodness and love.

John the Baptist's Choice Was Crucial for the Fate of Israel

Keeping in mind that every individual human being is called to fulfill his or her own responsibility and to follow what his or her conscience asks, we cannot consider that John the Baptist was the only one to blame for Jesus not being welcomed in his time, because there were many other religious leaders who met Jesus. Nevertheless, because God had raised John to such a highly regarded position and because he stood on the foundation of many righteous ancestors, his mistake affected the decisions of others. With John's denial of Jesus a cloud of darkness came upon all of Israel and the religious leaders.

This means, John the Baptist's choice was crucial for the fate of Israel, as well as for the fate of humanity. When he failed, he took all the priesthood and subsequently all the nation of Israel with him, bringing new sufferings and hardships to Israel while the world continued to remain in darkness. When there was no longer anyone who could respond to him, Jesus sadly cried out in Mt 23:35-38, *"And so upon you will come all the righteous blood that has been shed on earth, from the blood of righteous Abel to the blood of Zechariah son of Berekiah, whom you murdered between the temple and the altar. I tell you the truth, all this will come upon this generation. O Je-rusalem, Jerusalem, you who kill the prophets and stone those sent to you, how often I have longed to gather your children together, as a hen gathers her chicks under her wings, but you were not will-ing. Look, your house is left to you desolate."* Jesus could sense God's grief of seeing His Son, whom God sent to remove the sin of humankind, being rejected over and over.

We can be sure that if John the Baptist could be with us today, he would encourage all religious leaders to not repeat his mistake. And if one of us could have the opportunity to meet the One upon whom all our hopes lie, John might whisper into our ear, "Follow what your conscience tells you." We might even feel someone physically pinching us, even though there is no one who can be seen with our eyes.

Follow the Flame in Our Heart

Since it was the sin in his flesh that stopped John the Baptist from obeying what he heard inside, in order to not repeat his mistake, instead of being intimidated by the fear our sin creates in us, we need to follow the flame of our heart that becomes ignited when we meet Christ. This flame will allow us to have the attitude described in Ps 23:4, *"Even though I walk through the valley of the shadow of death, I will fear no evil, for you are with me; your rod and your staff they comfort me."* Therefore, when we meet Christ, we need to not be afraid of the love that passes through us for him and to allow ourselves to be guided by the feeling that is given to us. This is the reason Jesus answered someone posing a question in the following way: *"'Teacher, what must I do to inherit eternal life?' 'What is written in the Law?' he* (Jesus) *replied. 'How do you read it?' He answered: 'Love the Lord your God with all your heart and with all your soul and with all your strength and with all your mind' and, 'Love your neighbor as yourself.' 'You have answered correctly,' Jesus replied. 'Do this and you will live.'"* (Lk 10:25-28)

Indeed, if John had followed the call of the love he felt for the Christ, he would have found himself going with the Christ. If he did so, instead of darkness and doubt coming upon him, he would have experienced deep happiness, and not just for a short moment, but a lasting happiness that would have stayed with him every day of his remaining life. And the words of Paul that are recorded in Ro 6:11-12 would have become a reality for John: *"In the same way, count your-selves dead to sin but alive to God in Christ Jesus. Therefore do not let sin reign in your mortal body so that you obey its evil desires."*

BE READY TO FINISH JOHN THE BAPTIST'S JOURNEY

In order to finish the journey that John the Baptist could not walk to the end, if indeed we have the incredible opportunity to meet the living Christ, we want to make sure that we welcome him. Then we will no longer be slaves to the sin in our bodies; instead, what previously seemed shameful to us, we will see as pure; where there was darkness, we will see light; what we saw as dull will become exciting; what was dead will come to life.

Therefore, let us welcome the feeling of love we feel for the Christ. It does not belong to us, but it comes from the God of Heaven for His Beloved Son. If we obey this feeling, we will be able to do what John the Baptist could not do after meeting Jesus at the Jordan River, which is to become a child in front of the Lord and follow him as his shepherd. As well, let us recognize the feeling of love we can experience when we meet the Christ, because such an emotion can only be felt towards the one who is the Son of God. Let us be grateful to know what love is. This love will make the sin that has been covering and imprisoning us, leave from us. Then for the first time we will be able to feel the love that we have been longing for and dreaming about, but could never experience thus far. It is not human love but divine love, and such love can only come from and pass towards the one who is beloved by God.

Let us keep in mind, in order to be able to find that love, we need to obey what Jesus asked in Mt 10:37-39: *"Anyone who loves his father or mother more than me is not worthy of me; anyone who loves his son or daughter more than me is not worthy of me; and anyone who does not take his cross and follow me is not worthy of me. Whoever finds his life will lose it, and whoever loses his life for my sake will find it."*

If indeed we can do that, other people will also be able to experience love through us and for us as well, portrayed in Mt 10:40-41 as: *"He who receives you receives me, and he who receives me receives the one who sent me. Anyone who receives a prophet because he is a prophet will receive a prophet's reward, and anyone who receives a righteous man because he is a righteous man will receive a righteous man's reward."*

So, let us be bold and humble and accept to welcome the One who removes the sin of this world. In this way we, too, can receive the grace of the One who was sent to us, and we, too, can receive the love of his Father.

www.ingramcontent.com/pod-product-compliance
Lightning Source LLC
Chambersburg PA
CBHW060949040426
42445CB00011B/1069